CHINA IN GLOBAL CAPITALISM

CHINA
IN GLOBAL CAPITALISM

Building International Solidarity
against Imperial Rivalry

Eli Friedman, Kevin Lin,
Rosa Liu, and Ashley Smith

Haymarket Books
Chicago, IL

Published in 2024 by
Haymarket Books
P.O. Box 180165
Chicago, IL 60618
773-583-7884
www.haymarketbooks.org
info@haymarketbooks.org

ISBN: 979-8-88890-100-7

Distributed to the trade in the US through Consortium Book Sales and Distribution (www.cbsd.com) and internationally through Ingram Publisher Services International (www.ingramcontent.com).

This book was published with the generous support of Lannan Foundation, Wallace Action Fund, and the Marguerite Casey Foundation.

Special discounts are available for bulk purchases by organizations and institutions. Please email info@haymarketbooks.org for more information.

Cover design by Eric Kerl.

Printed in Canada by union labor.

Library of Congress Cataloging-in-Publication data is available.

10 9 8 7 6 5 4 3 2 1

CONTENTS

ACKNOWLEDGMENTS

Among the many scholars and activists—too many to name—that have inspired us, we'd particularly like to mention Adrian Budd, Tom Bramble, the Critical China Scholars, April Holcombe, Brian Hioe, Charlie Hore, Promise Li, Freya Putt, Pierre Rousset, JS Tan, Alex Tom, and Au Loong-Yu for their feedback and insights. Thanks as well to colleagues, friends, and partners for tolerating late night meetings and being a source of calm in the storm! And a special thanks to Anthony Arnove, Julie Fain, John McDonald, and the entire team at Haymarket Books. Of course, all mistakes and omissions are our own. But without the solidarity of this network of comrades and collaborators, this book would not have been possible.

INTRODUCTION

From trade wars and pandemic politics to rioting workers, intercontinental balloons, and battles over digital technology, contemporary China and its engagement with the world often appears conflictual and volatile. Internationally, China's relationship with the great powers, and particularly the United States, has become increasingly hostile in recent years. The US has moved from the overtly racist rhetoric and aggressive trade actions of the Trump years to a more buttoned-down but equally antagonistic effort by the Biden administration to coordinate with allies on technology, military, and economics to kneecap China's rise. Since Xi Jinping came to power in 2012, the Chinese state has intensified repression against dissent of all kinds, from the Uyghurs and Tibetans to Hong Kong protesters, human rights lawyers, labor activists, and feminists, all while increasing military aggression against Taiwan and in the South China Sea. A seemingly endless cycle of ratcheting nationalism, jingoism, and reactionary politics on both sides of the Pacific suggests a downward spiral that could plausibly result in catastrophic military confrontation.

Rather than a redux of the Cold War, it is the US-China capitalist *consensus* and intertwining that continues to generate such severe political instability and conflict. On both sides of the Pacific, respective political and military elites are trying to win domestic support for their zero-sum struggle to control the profits of a sputtering capitalist system. Shrinking sources of growth and stagnating

1

economic opportunities in most countries (including Europe and East Asia) have destabilized established patterns of life, resulting in increasing nationalism and xenophobia amid growing nostalgia for an imagined past of imperial glory. Of particular importance has been the sharpening of long-standing anti-Asian, and specifically anti-Chinese, racism in the US and the West more broadly. These domestic dynamics have been projected into the world via violent policing of human movement, trade battles, and militarism. Nonetheless, these destructive tendencies have also been met with widespread resistance. Within the People's Republic of China (PRC) and on its periphery, demands for ecological justice, economic redistribution, expanded rights for migrants, women, workers, and queer people, as well as movements for democracy, self-determination, and indigenous autonomy, all resonate with political currents globally.

In this short book, we lay out the global backdrop of interimperial rivalry in tandem with an account of Chinese people's resistance in order to help the international left think about how to engage with movements fighting for progressive causes within China. Our position is fundamentally animated by the belief that working-class and socially marginalized people of all nations share a common interest in opposing the *global* capitalist system that is predicated on class exploitation, racial and gender oppression, and ecological destruction. This book details China's social problems while contextualizing daily domestic and international political dramas within a broader historical and structural framework. Critically, we attempt to put forward ideas and strategies to advance an emancipatory and anti-capitalist political vision that can transcend rigidifying geopolitical boundaries. We draw out actually existing transnational connections and dynamics to demonstrate that international solidarity not only is possible, but that a radical reorganization of social and economic life *globally* is the only escape route from the very real possibility of war and ecological collapse.

We believe this intervention is necessary as the international left, broadly conceived, has not come to terms with China's dramatic impact on global capitalism and remains in a state of disarray over how to interpret these events. The most powerful, and therefore potentially dangerous, segment is the mainstream liberals who have allied with the right to advance Cold War–style rhetoric and policies. Articulated repeatedly and forcefully by the Biden administration, this position imagines the US state as the defender of global freedom and democracy pitted against a rising authoritarian tide led by China (but also including Russia, Iran, North Korea, Venezuela, and others). Many people in this camp are correct in their assessment that the Chinese state is guilty of massive human rights violations—but they identify the *source* of those problems as something unique to that state and they believe it can only be countered by forceful action by the US and other liberal democracies. They are incapable of interrogating the linkages between, for instance, Uyghur mass internment and the US-led global War on Terror or the exploitation of Chinese migrant workers by Chinese companies producing commodities for US brands, because the nominally liberal world order is directly implicated in these problems.

Some leftists have been drawn to a different pole that combines currents from both the left and right, which we might characterize as unidimensional anti-imperialism. The rather narrow band of agreement that ties them together is opposition to the US federal government—a position that is understandable, given the horrors perpetrated by the American empire over many decades. Nonetheless, where this view goes astray is the *sole* focus on social problems that derive from the actions of the American hegemon. While they are generally not avowedly pro-China (or pro-Russia), they shy away from judgment of oppressive or imperialist actions by the US's geopolitical rivals. 2023's "Rage Against the War Machine" event, while focused largely on Russia and Ukraine, was an excellent distillation of the political shortcomings of this position. The speaker list at this event included conservative "MAGA communist" Jackson Hinkle, self-described crypto entrepreneur Tatiana Moroz, Grayzone editor Max Blumenthal, as well as politicians such as Jill Stein, Dennis Kucinich, and Ron Paul.[1]

Although there are some prominent members in this political constellation, they lack institutional power and are largely composed of media personalities. While they are correct in their assessment that the US military and federal government are guilty of heinous crimes, they do not have an adequate analysis of the operation of capitalism as a *global* system of class exploitation and social oppression upheld and enforced by an array of state, corporate, and military actors. Furthermore, the notion that the world's ills can be solely attributed to US imperialism is increasingly implausible in a context where that very imperial might is in obvious decline. The fading of American unipolarity opens possibilities for advancing progressive aims, but it also means that other powerful actors in global capitalism (including China) are increasingly responsible for ongoing human suffering.

There is also a small group of avowedly pro-CCP (Chinese Communist Party) socialists or communists. This grouping argues that China represents not only a challenge to the US empire, but a systemic alternative to capitalism. In contrast to unidimensional anti-imperialists, they actively support the Chinese state and believe that it is building a postcapitalist society that has resulted in genuine human flourishing. This current consists of diasporic ethnonationalists, various sectarian leftists, and a vocal online community. The ethnonationalists are the only intellectually coherent thread of this group, as they are consistent in supporting the restoration of Chinese imperial might (whether or not this is a leftist position is another question). We think there is much to be learned from China's twentieth-century revolutions and understand the symbolic appeal of a self-proclaimed socialist state actively challenging the US empire today. Nonetheless, the argument that China is building an emancipatory socialism outside of capitalism is not grounded in reality, as will become clear in the chapters that follow. As a political organizing strategy, trying to persuade people in the US or China that uncritical support for the Chinese state will advance their struggles for freedom is obviously a nonstarter.

All three of these perspectives share a common blind spot: they overlook the ability of social movements to change the basic coordinates of power within which states operate. While the liberals can only relate to movements within China in an opportunistic way, in the hope that domestic discord harms China's development, the unidimensional anti-imperialists and pro-CCP left are either indifferent or actively hostile to Chinese people's demands for justice. And all three groups are united by their enthrallment to state power. If the state is seen as the only actor capable of exercising agency, we are left with the bleak choice of picking one side of the capitalist rivalry: Washington or Beijing.

Finally, many leftists—perhaps most—do not fall squarely into any of these groups, but rather are genuinely curious about how to interpret China's rise in a way that is consistent with their values. Many have misgivings about China's repressive politics, gaping economic inequalities, and massive CO_2 emissions, but do not want to endorse the increasingly Sinophobic imperialism emanating from Washington. Within this context it is understandable when many are cautious about entering the political fray. In fact, the left already has a set of principles that can serve as a guide to understanding China and its relationship with the world in the twenty-first century. These include commitments to realizing radical democracy, environmental justice, and economies organized around human need, while ending social hierarchies based on race, gender, sexuality, and ability.

Figuring out how to apply these principles outside of the more familiar terrain of the West can be hard work, and it means challenging many assumptions we have inherited from the history of the Cold War and the cycle of national liberation struggles in the twentieth century. But our observations in universities, the labor movement, and other left-wing political spaces are that most people are keenly interested in thinking through the epochal changes affected by China's rise and how best to advance social emancipation within rapidly shifting geopolitical conditions. Our greatest wish is to play some role in advancing these discussions.

The initial impetus for this book came when some of the authors organized a daylong event in January 2020, the proceedings of which have been published by Verso Books as *The China Question*.[2] At the time, we were alarmed by the rapid escalation of rabidly nationalist rhetoric and action under Donald Trump and the increasingly dictatorial political turn China had taken under Xi Jinping. Furthermore, it seemed as though the US left, and the international left more broadly, was unable to make sense of important recent events in China, notably the mass internment of the Uyghurs and Hong Kong's generalized social insurgency in 2019. In the years since, the left's need to grapple with the China question has only become more pressing for several reasons. First, there is now a strong bipartisan commitment in the US federal government to contain China's rise, which has led to an ongoing series of legislative and administrative actions. As sclerotic and dysfunctional as US politics have become, the federal government has mustered fearsome coordinated action in response to China's growing power. This in turn has only strengthened the hand of nationalistic elements in the CCP, as there is plenty of evidence that the US will not abide a powerful China.

Second, this deteriorating political relationship between states has undercut the neoliberal consensus forged in the 1990s. Both the US and China have turned toward increasing state intervention into their economies with dueling industrial and protectionist policies. Absent direct military conflict, full economic decoupling is out of the question, but there has been immense pressure put on global supply chains that were predicated on the ideology of separating politics from economics. Even if Euro-American corporations continue to benefit from exploiting Chinese workers for many years, they are hedging their bets and increasingly sourcing from friendlier nations such as Mexico, Vietnam, and India. In essence, national security concerns are playing a much larger role in the organization of production within global capitalism. This process has been accelerated by the trade war's tariffs as well as the US's growing list of technologies subject to an export ban to China.

Third, militarization of the Indo-Pacific region has advanced to a frightening extent in recent years. China has continued to build out bases in contested waters in the South China Sea, while its military technology and spending continue to expand. The Biden administration has fortified the Quad (Australia, India, Japan, US) while forming the new AUKUS military alliance (Australia,

UK, US). Japan is in a process of remilitarization, South Korea has floated the idea of developing nuclear weapons, and the US has a new agreement to allow for troop rotations at several locations in the Philippines. Taiwan remains the most likely flashpoint. China launched an overwhelming display of military force across the strait following Nancy Pelosi's visit in the summer of 2022, and has continued to employ stepped-up gray zone tactics around the island. All of these recent developments have further reinforced the need for a consistent anti-imperialist *and* internationalist response to the twenty-first century's defining rivalry.

This book explains transformations in Chinese and global capitalism that have led us to this conjuncture. It is organized as follows: Part 1 begins by establishing that China is capitalist in every meaningful sense, and then details its rise through the global system. Understanding China's role in global capitalism is a key building block for the rest of the book, as it allows us to understand both the dynamics of its internal social problems and collective resistance, as well as the state's behavior domestically and internationally. Part 2 provides an account of China's domestic social conditions, analyzing various forms of exploitation and oppression as well as resistance by workers, peasants, women, and ethnic minorities. This includes a discussion of China's fractious periphery, including Tibet and Xinjiang as well as Hong Kong and Taiwan.

Part 3 shifts to the international political arena and explains why we characterize the US-China relationship as an interimperial rivalry. We then discuss climate change and the pandemic, as these phenomena can only be adequately understood and addressed from a global perspective. In the final section of the book, we turn to thinking concretely about how to organize international solidarity at a time of growing geopolitical conflict. This entails a discussion of the role of the Chinese diaspora as well as the economic linkages and points of leverage that might bring working-class people together across and against the imperial divide.

PART I

THE RISE OF CHINESE CAPITALISM

CHAPTER 1

CHINA IS CAPITALIST

Twenty-first-century China is capitalist. This fact represents a dramatic transformation for a country that had basically eliminated private ownership of the means of production by the end of the 1950s, while engaging in some of the twentieth century's most radical political experiments during the following decade. Despite the profound reorganization of property relations over the past forty years, the Communist Party (CCP) retains its monopoly on power and still claims to be socialist, albeit now with "Chinese characteristics." China's road to capitalism[1] has led to serious confusion within the left (both within China and globally) about how to understand the nature of the country and its economic system. Clarifying this issue is critically important for anti-capitalist practice, and it is made all the more so by China's increasing global power.

There are two key reasons why this analysis is significant. First, as we will see in subsequent chapters, the emerging conflict with the US is profoundly shaped by the pressures of global capitalist competition. Mistaking this as an "ideological" struggle between socialism and capitalism (or authoritarianism vs. democracy) would lead to analytical and strategic dead-ends. As just one example, an "ideological struggle" framework proves useless in explaining the recent tit-for-tat technology war that has seen the US ban the export of a range of advanced semiconductors and semiconductor production hardware, while China has responded by controlling the export of gallium and germanium, two metals used in a range of high technology components. The US is not limiting technology exports out of a concern for democracy—its autocratic allies from Saudi Arabia to Singapore are free to purchase these items.

On the other hand, China is clearly pursuing leadership in 5G, AI, and semiconductors so it can capture a growing share of the global market, and its limiting the export of key metals is to damage US firms rather than to advance socially responsive technology. Interstate conflict is being driven significantly by political elites' desire to secure profitability for their respective corporations. In the case of the US, this includes capitalists from countries within its imperial umbrella, such as the EU, Australia, South Korea, and Japan, whereas for China it is more nationally bounded. We need to be crystal clear that the Chinese state's opposition to the US-led order is about asserting its interests in global capitalism, *not* advancing a socially emancipatory politics against that system.

The second reason is that China's capitalist character must inform our understanding of and relationship to social resistance in the country. Once we grasp that the state governs in the general interest of capital, we can comprehend the dynamics of labor unrest, citizens protesting environmental harm, feminists fighting workplace discrimination and harassment, peasants resisting dispossession, and ethnic minorities suffering displacement and unfree labor. These movements confront the Chinese state as a hostile power precisely because it is a hyper-nationalist, patriarchal, and capitalist state. As is true for every country, China has its particular history and set of social and political characteristics that influence patterns of resistance and containment. Nonetheless, it shares core attributes of all other states within global capitalism, and these provide the basis of common material interests between Chinese workers and oppressed groups with their siblings throughout the world, including the US. These interests open the possibility for building international solidarity among movements in capitalist countries against our common ruling-class enemies.

CHINESE CAPITALISM, CLASS EXPLOITATION, AND SOCIAL REPRODUCTION

Capitalism is a system in which the owners of corporations exploit workers' labor in competition with other corporations to make the most profit. Capital's compulsion to accumulate takes precedence over meeting human needs, as the natural world is treated as an object to plunder regardless of consequences to the environment, while workers are forced into the market to purchase the goods they need to survive. The competitive drive for endless accumulation drives corporations into conflict with each other, forcing them to innovate, invest in research and development, squeeze higher productivity out of their workers, and make them work longer and harder for lower wages.

This economic exploitation of working-class labor for profit structures class inequality and is always interwoven with oppressions of race, gender, and nation. To enforce these inequalities, the system requires a state to enforce capital's rule, reproduce it, and ensure its profitability, including against other capitalist states and their corporations. Thus, competition among corporations leads to economic, diplomatic, and even military conflict among states for dominance over global capitalism. China possesses all of these attributes, despite also having political and economic differences with the liberal Anglo-American model of capitalism.

Indicators of Chinese capitalism abound. The country's metropolises are adorned with luxury stores selling Ferraris and Gucci, foreign and domestic corporate logos are emblazoned across the skyline, and high-rise luxury housing has sprouted in the urban core. It has evolved from one of the most economically equal countries in the world into one of the most unequal.[2] China's state has embraced global capitalism: it joined the World Trade Organization (WTO); insists that it is a market economy;[3] and Xi Jinping has defended globalization in Davos[4] and advocated for the market to play a "decisive role" in resource allocation.[5] Similarly, one can find widespread cultural expressions typical of capitalist societies, including the valorization of hard work, celebration of crass consumerism, and glorification of corporate profitability as sources of national pride. It would, however, be a mistake to confuse such effects of capitalism with capitalism itself. It is necessary to probe more deeply into the nature of China's state and economy in order to demonstrate their capitalist nature.

One way to do that is to determine how and why things are produced. Marx begins *Capital* with an analysis of the commodity form because he believed it would allow us to unlock the entirety of the capitalist system. When looking at contemporary China, there is no question that the things people need to survive and flourish are produced as commodities. This is apparent in the vast transnational supply chains that are centered in China, where the exploitation of Chinese workers in factories producing everything from cell phones and cars to medical equipment, garments, and furniture has enriched corporations both domestic and foreign, while resulting in an export boom of unprecedented proportions.[6] Chinese tech giants such as Tencent, Alibaba, Baidu, and ByteDance are distinct from Silicon Valley firms in some important ways, but they are united in their efforts to produce technology that is oriented, first and foremost, toward the commodification of information. Similarly, recurrent real estate bubbles and massive private development companies show that housing is produced in response to market opportunities.[7] Across a wide variety of sectors, it is clear that production of commodities for the sake of profit governs the economy, not production for human need.

The capitalist nature of society is most evident from the standpoint of its proletariat, the working class whose only productive property is their own labor power. Just as in other capitalist societies, proletarians in China must find a job in order to pay for commodities to meet their basic needs. Items such as food, housing, education, health care, transportation, and time for leisure and socializing are not provided by the government. Rather, the vast majority of people in China must sell their labor power—their ability to work—to private or state-owned corporations in return for a wage in order to pay for necessities. The position of China's migrant labor force is illustrative of the general pattern. Over the last few decades, nearly three hundred million migrant workers have left their towns and villages, where they have official household registration (*hukou*), to form a gargantuan labor force at the base of China's industrial transformation. Once a migrant worker leaves their place of *hukou* registration, they forsake any right to state-subsidized programs and services, effectively rendering them second-class citizens within their own country. The only reason hundreds of millions of people would make this "choice" is because they cannot survive in the impoverished rural areas and are compelled by market forces to seek work in the urban centers.

The appearance of the capitalist labor market was politically contentious in the late 1970s, as many in the CCP still supported the Maoist "iron rice bowl" system of lifetime employment. Although wages were paltry under this system, urban workers in most enterprises had free or nearly free access to housing, education, and health care. Most importantly, it was nearly impossible to remove people from their employment. While consumption was repressed and life was not luxurious, this subset of the population enjoyed high social status and strong social protections. But by the 1990s the state had clearly decided that capitalist labor markets were the future, signaled most clearly by 1994's Labor Law, which established a legal framework for wage labor.

This meant establishing a basis for labor contracts (which did not exist under the iron rice bowl system), allowing municipalities to set minimum wages, regulating labor disputes through a system of mediation, arbitration, and litigation, and building a patchwork system of employment-based insurance. Rather than ushering in a highly regulated labor market in the social democratic mold (as many reformers wanted), however, labor has been commodified and remains highly informal.[8] Even after the implementation of 2008's Labor Contract Law, which was specifically focused on increasing legal labor contracts, the number of migrant workers with contracts *fell* over the course of the early 2010s, with only 35.1 percent having coverage as of 2016.[9]

Workers without a contract do not enjoy legal protections, making it extremely difficult to address labor rights violations.

Furthermore, social insurance—including health insurance, pensions, workplace injury insurance, unemployment, and "birth insurance"—is employer-based for migrant workers. Being relegated to labor informality produces other forms of exclusion and market dependence for migrants. If, for instance, they want to enroll their children in an urban public school, they are required to produce a local labor contract—a stipulation that does not apply to urban residents with local household registration. As a majority of migrant workers do not have local labor contracts, this results in a highly socially differentiated system of education. Although the mechanisms for distributing nominally public goods such as education vary widely by city, the general logic is to privilege those that the state has determined are useful in upgrading the local economy.[10] Many large cities have "point-based" plans in which applicants must accumulate points based on a series of labor market–oriented metrics (e.g., highest level of education, skill certifications, "model worker" awards) in order to access public services. Everyone else is left to the whims of the market.

The situation for urban proletarians who work in the same place as their *hukou* registration is somewhat different, and certainly better from a material standpoint. They can access public schooling, possibly some housing subsidies, and are much more likely to have a legally binding labor contract. Welfare benefits in China are not generous, and social spending as a share of GDP is far below the OECD (Organization for Economic Co-operation and Development) average,[11] but urban residents in their *hukou* area can secure them. That said, there are deep class and regional inequities as well as fiscal problems that plague the system.[12] As a result, there is no question that even these relatively privileged groups are compelled to sell their labor power to capitalists in order to secure adequate health care, decent housing, or security in retirement.

The *dibao* program, a security net that purportedly guarantees a minimum livelihood, is neither sufficient nor intended to support reproduction at a socially acceptable level.[13] Like all welfare systems, benefits are kept low enough to compel workers to get jobs for a better life. Xi Jinping himself made his position on social protections clear in 2021 when he said, "Even if our level of development is higher in the future and finances are more abundant, we cannot set too high a goal and have excessive guarantees. We must resolutely guard against falling into the trap of supporting lazy people through 'welfarism.'"[14]

THE CAPITALIST NATURE OF THE CHINESE STATE

Not only is China's economy capitalist, but its state rules in the general interest of capital. That does not mean that the state serves all capitalists in the same way; like all capitalist states, it balances among various corporations in an attempt to preserve the overall profitability and growth of the economy. In some cases, it infringes on the interests of particular capitalists (as with the 2021 crackdown on big tech), while in other cases it subsidizes them, all in what they judge is the overall interest of the system at any one time. The Chinese state has its own relative autonomy like other capitalist states.

The state's capitalist nature is abundantly clear in shop floor politics. China has seen an explosion of worker insurgency over the past three decades; the country is the global leader in wildcat strikes.[15] How does the state respond when workers employ the time-honored tradition of withholding their labor from capital? Its police intervene almost exclusively on behalf of the bosses against workers, a service they provide to private domestic, foreign, and state-owned enterprises alike. There are innumerable instances in which police or state-sponsored thugs have used coercion to break a strike. One particularly prominent example was the violent police suppression of the strike of forty thousand workers at the Taiwanese-owned Yue Yuen shoe factory in 2014. The workers noted the historical irony of China's riot cops intervening on behalf of Taiwanese capitalists, whose government Beijing opposes. If the strike elegantly poses the question, "Which side are you on?," the Chinese state has made it clear it is on the side of the bosses.

State violence has also been deployed in the policing of informal workers in urban public space. The much-hated *chengguan*—a para-police force formed in 1997 for the purpose of enforcing non-criminal regulations—has on countless occasions employed shockingly coercive methods to clear street hawkers and other informal workers from the street. Such police brutality has generated a deep and widespread animosity among the country's informal workers, and anti-*chengguan* riots have been common. In perhaps the most spectacular and violent example, migrant workers in Zengcheng, Guangdong, took to the streets en masse in 2011 when a rumor spread that a pregnant woman had miscarried after being assaulted during a *chengguan* operation. After days of widespread rioting, the People's Liberation Army violently put down the insurrection.[16]

There are other important ways that the state represents the interests of capital in politically subjugating workers, implementing constitutional changes, imposing laws, and restricting labor rights. In 1982, just as the PRC started enacting free-market reforms, Deng Xiaoping removed the right to strike from the constitution. The only legal union is the All-China Federation of Trade Unions (ACFTU), an organization that is controlled by CCP. Rather than representing workers and defending their interests, the ACFTU ensures labor peace for corporations. Unsurprisingly, it is standard practice for enterprise HR managers to be appointed as the chair for the company-level union. It goes without saying that workers do not see ACFTU unions as serving their interests, and when they attempt to build autonomous organizations as an alternative they are met with harsh repression. One recent example comes from the spring of 2021, when activist Chen Guojiang was arrested for his efforts to organize food delivery workers to demand fair treatment from the gargantuan tech companies that employ them.[17]

The political subjugation of the proletariat extends to formal state structures as well as civil society. All citizens, including workers, have no right to self-organize in civil society, form political parties, or vote in elections, so they are entirely dependent on the goodwill of the CCP to represent them. But the Party does not claim to represent *only* the interests of workers and peasants. Since admitting capitalists to the Party and advancing the concept of "Three Represents" under Jiang Zemin, they now claim to represent the "fundamental interests of the overwhelming majority of the people of China."

In combination with the state's de facto ban on acknowledging class antagonism,[18] it is clear that the social basis of one-party rule has undergone a profound transformation. A cursory assessment of the social makeup of the central government reveals not just that capital has good access to state power, but it is also fundamentally *inseparable* from state power. By the 1998–2003 session of the National People's Congress (NPC), workers made up just 1 percent of representatives, while entrepreneurs constituted 20.5 percent, a stark reversal from the 1970s.[19] Today, the NPC and Chinese People's Political Consultative Congress have an astonishing concentration of plutocrats. In 2018, the wealthiest 153 members of these two central government bodies had an estimated combined wealth of USD $650 billion.[20] The legislature has sought to incorporate people who made billions in the private sector, such as Pony Ma, head of internet giant Tencent.

There is now a revolving door between Chinese corporate power and official positions in state institutions. Ironically, this seamless exchange is not all that different than in other capitalist states like the US. And government bureaucrats take advantage of their position to become private capitalists. For example, the family of Wen Jiabao (the former premier) leveraged their political connections to build personal wealth estimated at USD $2.7 billion.[21] In twenty-first-century China, capital begets political power just as political power begets capital. "Socialism" for party bureaucrats means nothing more than state involvement in managing the economy and their own self-preservation.

CAPITALISM AND STATE OWNERSHIP

State ownership of corporations must not be confused with socialism. In fact, state ownership of the economy can function in a capitalist manner. As Friedrich Engels argued in *Anti-Dühring*, "The modern state, whatever its form, is an essentially capitalist machine; it is the state of the capitalists, the ideal collective body of all capitalists. The more productive forces it takes over as its property, the more it becomes the real collective body of all the capitalists, the more citizens it exploits. The workers remain wage-workers, proletarians. The capitalist relationship is not abolished; it is rather pushed to an extreme."[22]

The key question to decide whether the state is capitalist or not is who controls the state, whose interests it serves, and what logic drives its state-owned industry. If workers control the state and use its power to address democratically determined social needs, then it makes sense to call it socialist. But if bureaucrats and capitalists control the state, use it to make profit, and competition is its underlying logic, it remains capitalist. The fact that avowedly capitalist states have controlled large parts of their own economies undermines the claim that state ownership can be equated with socialism, and, as we will see, China's state-owned enterprises (SOEs) are not fundamentally different from those in many other countries. Today, bureaucratic capitalists in China control the state and use its ownership and control over SOEs to enhance the global competitiveness of its national economy and corporations.

There is no doubt that Chinese state intervention in the economy is more extensive than is the case in most other countries. But, before the current neoliberal period in which privatization became common, SOEs were a common feature of many capitalist societies. During the mid-20th century, for example, state-owned industries were widespread in Europe, India, and even Kuomintang-controlled Taiwan, where SOEs contributed nearly one quarter of the country's GDP as late as the 1980s.[23] Today, state-owned Saudi Aramco is number six on the *Fortune* Global 500, and it continues to play a leading role in advancing ecological catastrophe.

In fact, as Ha-Joon Chang has demonstrated in several books, including *Kicking Away the Ladder*,[24] late developing capitalist economies have always used state ownership and state protectionism in attempting to establish capitalist corporations and to ensure their competitiveness. Even the US did so when it won independence from Britain. Later, during the Second World War, the federal government subordinated private capital to the dictates of the war economy, financed corporate investment, and set prices and wages. State intervention oriented toward enhancing efficiency, profitability, and predictability is not antithetical to capitalism, but has been and is still a strategy states use to ensure their economic stability, competitiveness, growth, and profitability.

CHINA'S CAPITALIST SOES

The capitalist nature of China's state ownership becomes patently obvious when looked at from the vantage point of the country's working class. From that perspective, the difference between state and private capital is minimal. Tens of millions of state-sector workers were laid off in the 1990s and early 2000s as part of the state's campaign to "smash the iron rice bowl."[25] Thrown into a labor market for which they were wholly unprepared, this privatization campaign engendered subsistence crises and massive class struggle.[26] Following this wave of sell-offs and theft of worker pensions, the remaining SOEs have been subjected to market forces, including in their labor regimes.[27] Global behemoths such as China National Petroleum and SAIC Motor have to compete in international markets against the likes of ExxonMobil and Toyota; the coercive power of the market leaves SOEs no choice but to squeeze more value out of their workers.

Like large or monopolistic firms in any capitalist country, Chinese SOE employees often have somewhat better compensation and job security than in more competitive sectors. But SOEs have also been particularly enthusiastic adopters of "dispatch" and temporary labor strategies, in large part because informal workers afford them greater flexibility. Furthermore, as sociologist Joel Andreas has extensively documented, the admittedly imperfect experiments with workplace democracy in the Mao era have been eviscerated by marketization, and SOE workers are now equally subordinate to management as in an equivalent private firm.[28] SOEs have been just as intolerant of independent unions as their private counterparts, and workers have no capacity to supervise or influence decisions in production. These firms are in no sense *public* property—they belong to and are controlled by an unaccountable state bureaucracy.

China's SOEs are also an increasingly important lynchpin of global capitalism and subject to its competitive pressures. Indeed, eighty-two of them were in the Fortune Global 500 in 2021.[29] Although the state retains controlling shares, SOEs have been allowed to list on stock exchanges in China and abroad, giving transnational capital at least a seat at the table. The three largest Chinese SOEs listed on American markets are China Life, PetroChina, and Sinopec, with a combined market capitalization of $312.6 billion.[30] Their lead underwriters include a who's who of global financial institutions: Credit Suisse, Citigroup, and Deutsche Bank for China Life; Blackrock, JP Morgan, Citigroup, and Goldman Sachs for PetroChina; and Morgan Stanley and China International Capital Corp for Sinopec. Even if these SOEs are distinct in many ways from private corporations, global capital would not be so heavily involved were they not convinced that there are profits to be made.

Many of China's largest state firms are not only engaged in their own profit-oriented activities, but they also work hand-in-glove with foreign capitalists. Following an agreement with the Trump administration, in 2021 China's largest bank ICBC established a wealth management joint venture with Goldman Sachs while the second-largest bank, China Construction Bank, did the same with Blackrock. This follows decades of joint ventures between SOEs and foreign corporations in a variety of industries, the most prominent of which is auto, where most foreign brands (e.g., GM, Toyota, Hyundai, Volkswagen) are represented. Foreign corporations are of course entering these joint ventures to access the highly profitable Chinese market.

Although not specific to SOEs, foreign capitalists have until quite recently been bullish on Chinese capitalism, even following its statist turn under Xi. While investment has shifted away from tech and education following government crackdowns in those sectors, 2021 witnessed a new record of US $65.5 billion in foreign investment pouring into China's Shenzhen and Shanghai equity markets. Even as China's economy was hampered by ongoing COVID lockdowns, US foreign direct investment in China increased by nine percent in 2022 to $126.1 billion.[31] It is apparent enough to such investors that the state's recent regulation of private enterprise is not an attack on capital in general; it is about redirecting flows of investment to priority industries.

Much controversy has surrounded the Belt and Road Initiative (discussed further in subsequent chapters), with many foreign detractors characterizing it as a form of "debt trap diplomacy." But there is scant evidence of any such geopolitical conspiracy. Rather, beginning in the early 2010s, the government encouraged firms—especially SOEs—to venture abroad to deal with growing industrial overcapacity by opening up and conquering new markets.

As is true for all nations in a position to extend credit to indebted nations, China's financial position comes with political leverage. But the primary impetus is to find an outlet for surplus capital, expand opportunities for profit making, ensure reliable access to natural resources, and build infrastructure that enhances China's centrality within global capitalism.

One clear example of this has been Chinese SOEs' enthusiastic embrace of construction projects in Israel. Chinese construction companies have been building a massive port in the southern city of Ashdod (just to the north of Gaza) as well as Tel Aviv's new light rail system. Similarly, as part of a privatization effort, in 2015 the Shanghai International Port Group won the right to expand and operate Israel's largest port in Haifa for twenty-five years. These state-owned companies are literally building the infrastructure of settler colonialism, not because the Chinese state has ordered them to abet the eradication of Palestine, but simply because Israel provides them with opportunities for profits. While China's SOEs are distinct from private firms in several respects, it is apparent enough they have little to do with socialism.

CAPITALIZATION OF LAND

The question of land is related to but distinct from SOEs. All urban land is owned by the state while all rural land is owned collectively by local residents. But as a huge volume of research has demonstrated, the separation of use rights from ownership rights has ushered in unmistakably capitalist uses of the earth's surface. In cities this produced a historically unprecedented boom in construction of housing as a commodity to be bought and sold on the market. Urban governments are highly fiscally dependent on the profits from land auctions, leading to a tight alignment of the local state bureaucracy's interests with those of developers. In 2023, the government began experimenting with property-focused private equity funds, specifically for the purpose of funneling foreign capital into the country's faltering real estate sector.[32] From financiers to construction equipment manufacturers and commodities exporters, profiting from China's real estate boom has become a global concern.

Rural *hukou* holders are entitled to a plot of land, though as mass rural-to-urban migration reveals, it is rarely enough or of sufficient quality to sustain social reproduction. Outward expansion of the city has resulted in mass dispossession of peasants. As with workers in SOEs, peasants have little ability to exercise supervision or control over their (nominally) collectively owned land, and the village leaders speak on behalf of the collective. The consequence has been endless cycles of land dispossession in which peasants generally receive a fraction of the market value of their land, while the state bureaucrats and capitalist developers cash in. Finally, for those people who do maintain rural land, agriculture in China has undergone a profound capitalist transformation, with land use rights being consolidated by agribusiness while inputs such as fertilizer and seeds are also commodified.[33] The fact that land is by right held collectively has done little to impede this process.

CHINESE CAPITALISM AND INTERNATIONAL SOLIDARITY

Thus, every facet of Chinese society is capitalist—its economy, its state, class relations, and social institutions. Understanding this fact is not merely an academic exercise, it has important practical consequences. The interimperial rivalry with the US is fundamentally, if not exclusively, a struggle over control of natural resources, technologies, markets, intellectual property—in short, the essential ingredients for ensuring competitive advantage, profitability, and power within global capitalism. Socialists have no side in this growing rivalry between the two powers.

Our solidarity must be with the workers and socially marginalized in both countries. Understanding that China is capitalist allows us to trace transnational points of convergence and solidarity with workers and oppressed people. The most obvious example is when workers are exploited by the same global corporations such as Walmart, Tesla, BYD, or other firms that have extensive operations in China, the US, and beyond. But there are more general processes driven by the logic of capital that produce similar conditions, and therefore possibilities for solidarity, across borders in struggles against gender, racial, and national oppression.

It is not coincidental that Chinese feminists quickly adopted the language of #MeToo to challenge their male bosses, or that the language of "lying flat," a form of passive resistance to market pressures, has resonated with young people far beyond China. Undocumented Mexican workers in the US and undocumented Vietnamese workers in southern China share an experience of exploitation and state repression, produced by the common logic of racialized border policing. And prisoners in the US and interned Muslims in Xinjiang are both subjected to regimes of racist carceral exploitation. We have much more in common with each other than we do with the political elites, bureaucrats, and capitalists of our respective nations. The task of the left is to make the intensifying capitalist rivalry and all of its grotesque manifestations a relic of history.

CHAPTER 2

THE EMERGENCE
OF A NEW GREAT POWER

n the 1970s, few would have predicted China's rise as a capitalist
power. But over the last four decades, it has transformed itself
from an autarchic, underdeveloped economy into a global economic force. Its rise is the most dramatic one in the history of the
capitalist system since the emergence of the US as an industrial and
imperial state at the beginning of the twentieth century. In 1978,
China only accounted for about 2 percent of the world economy.[1]
Now it is the second biggest economy in the world, the largest exporter, the number-one trade partner of most of the world's major economies, a major exporter of capital, and a top recipient of
foreign direct investment (FDI). It is determined to move up the
global value chain to become a high-tech competitor with the established titans of the world economy like the US, Germany, Japan,
and others.

Based on this rapid ascent, China has become a new imperial
power with all the qualities of its rivals, albeit with its own distinct
characteristics. It battles for its share of the world market, rein-
forces the underdevelopment of the Global South, and cuts deals
to secure resources throughout the world. China's integration into
global capitalism has generated both collaboration and competition
between it and the US as well as the other imperialist powers. On
the one hand, China depends on them for investment, markets,

and technology, but on the other hand, it comes into conflict with them, especially the US, as it tries to leap up the value chain.

China, however, is different from the other economic heavyweights. Unlike Germany or Japan, it is outside the security infrastructures and alliances that the US built during the Cold War. This geopolitical independence combined with its state ownership of key industries as well as its state management of private capital provide it greater latitude than Washington's allies, who are all subordinated to the United State's economic, political, and military institutions. Especially since the Great Recession, China has found itself at loggerheads with the US over everything from trade to high-tech, geopolitics, and military dominance in the Asia Pacific. President Xi Jinping has broken with his cautious predecessors, who were reluctant to openly proclaim their imperial ambitions, to declare China's status as a great power in a multipolar world order.

UNDERDEVELOPMENT AND PRIMITIVE ACCUMULATION

Today's China was established through revolutionary struggle against imperialism. In the nineteenth and early twentieth centuries, the world's imperialist powers including Britain, France, Germany, Russia, and Japan imposed their will on the old, imperial China, which could not resist their predation. The Qing Empire was toppled in a revolution in 1911, but the new Republic of China failed to stabilize the country, which fell prey to civil war. Japan took advantage of that chaos to invade and seize Manchuria in 1931, setting up a puppet government that oversaw a reign of terror. Two competing forces rose up to challenge the occupation—Chiang Kai-shek's pro-capitalist Kuomintang (KMT) and Mao Zedong's Chinese Communist Party. The KMT crushed the CCP-led left in 1927, and imposed its rule throughout much of the country. Nevertheless, starting in the 1930s the CCP collaborated with the KMT in a war to drive Japan out of the country, which they finally did in 1945.

Over the next four years, the two waged a civil war that the CCP won decisively, driving the KMT from the mainland to Taiwan where it imposed dictatorial rule. On the mainland, the CCP founded the People's Republic of China (PRC) in 1949. Soon, Mao's new regime abolished private property and placed the economy under state and collective ownership. To overcome the country's destitution, it imitated Joseph Stalin's Soviet Union, pursuing state-led development of its national economy disconnected from global capitalism. This was not a choice, but a necessity forced on it by its position as an underdeveloped country faced with hostile imperialists, especially the US, which it confronted over Taiwan and fought in the Korean War in the 1950s. Like other late developers, China used its state to protect its economy from international competition, prevent its subordination to the great powers, and develop its national economic capacity.

It initially focused on investment in its industrial infrastructure to build military armaments, including nuclear weapons.[2] But, isolated from the world economy and unable to get the support it wanted from its nominal ally, the USSR, the new state exploited workers and especially peasants to squeeze a surplus out of them to invest in development. Although there were important gains in terms of health and education, particularly for women, the state repressed consumption, at best providing relatively egalitarian poverty in the countryside and cities. By concentrating surpluses extracted largely from the peasantry, the PRC carried out a version of what Marx called the primitive accumulation of capital.[3]

The CCP's first five-year plan in the 1950s rapidly industrialized the country, establishing key industries like steel as pillars of the economy. Between 1953 and 1957, it grew at an astonishing pace of 19 percent a year.[4] Amid this stunning expansion, China joined other newly independent states at the Bandung Conference in 1955 to launch the nonaligned movement with the hope of blazing a path of Third World development. But China was starting at such a deficit that even with rapid growth it fell further behind both the Western states and the USSR, which it split from in the early 1960s.

To overcome this backwardness, Mao abandoned five-year planning to launch the Great Leap Forward, a voluntarist attempt to rush the pace of development by encouraging peasants to carry out rural industrialization by building backyard steel mills and large-scale irrigation projects. This ended in catastrophe. The mills produced unusable, poor-quality steel, and the mismanagement of agriculture helped precipitate a famine, leading to the deaths of some 30 million people.[5] Instead of catching up, China found itself even more deeply trapped in underdevelopment as its imperial rivals boomed throughout the 1960s.[6]

The rest of the bureaucracy sidelined Mao and returned to more cautious five-year planning. But, as before, that continued to fail in closing the gap between China and its more advanced rivals. Frustrated with this impasse, Mao ignited the Cultural Revolution in 1966. He encouraged and used the struggles of students, workers, and peasants to reclaim authority over the CCP against his bureaucratic rivals. But the uprising escaped Mao's ability to control it, with strikes erupting in the country's industrial center in Shanghai and elsewhere. With the regime's rule threatened from below, Mao turned to the army to reimpose order. After the chaos of the Cultural Revolution, the country was left more destitute and isolated than ever before.[7] To escape China's developmental cul-de-sac, Mao struck an alliance with the US against the USSR during President Richard Nixon's famous visit to China in 1972.

DENG XIAOPING'S INTEGRATION OF CHINA INTO GLOBAL CAPITALISM

After Mao's death in 1976 and another fierce factional battle in the bureaucracy for control of the state, Deng Xiaoping secured leadership of the CCP. He launched what he called a "Second Revolution" to abandon autarchic national development and replace it with state-managed integration with global capitalism. While he maintained party-state dictatorship and state ownership of key industries, he started to introduce market reforms into the economy, creating the space for the development of private capital. His model for the new strategy was other states in the region, the so-called Asian Tigers, like South Korea, who selected and backed corporations as "national champions" to develop their national economies through manufacturing products for export to the world market.

To implement this new strategy, Deng introduced his "Four Modernizations" in agriculture, industry, science and technology, and defense. He devolved planning to regional and local governments, allowed those to carry out rural industrialization through the "Township and Village Enterprises" to produce for the market, opened agriculture to private use with the household responsibility system, began the process of introducing the market into state-owned urban industries, and opened Special Economic Zones (SEZs) for multinational investment in the country's coastal cities. With these market reforms, labor and its products became commodities bought and sold in an emergent capitalist market, one increasingly part of the world system. Deng hoped these changes would encourage FDI and technology transfer to fuel further expansion of the Chinese economy. His new strategy would unleash four decades of economic expansion, during which China averaged double-digit annual growth, transforming the country into the new workshop of the world. This rapid accumulation has been premised on the exploitation of the country's new migrant working class, drawn from its massive rural reserve army of labor inherited from the Mao era.

Like all capitalist economies, China has been subject to the system's contradictions, its patterns of uneven and combined development, and its booms as well as its crises. To manage these, the state bureaucracy has vacillated between emphasizing state control and increasing the opening to the international market. China hit the first of its many crises at the end of the 1980s. Deng's market reforms triggered inflation and with that a host of economic grievances among peasants and workers, as well as hopes for democratization among students and intellectuals. These detonated the vast uprising in Tiananmen Square and elsewhere, which the bureaucracy suppressed with the utmost brutality in June 1989 to avoid the fate of Eastern European rulers who were toppled the same year.[8]

ACCELERATING INTEGRATION INTO GLOBAL CAPITALISM

This violent repression isolated China for a period, as the imperialist powers and their corporations paused their relations and investment. The ongoing flow of funds from the rest of Asia, especially Hong Kong and Taiwan, made up for these losses. Amid this renewed isolation, sections of the bureaucracy considered abandoning market reforms. By contrast, Deng campaigned to double down on them and open the economy to global capitalism even more radically. He conducted his famous Southern Tour in 1992, in which he reaffirmed that SEZs in cities like Shenzhen were the best way to lure much-needed FDI and fuel a new cycle of development.

The timing could not have been better; China opened up at the same time as states and multinationals turned to neoliberal globalization to restore growth and profitability. After abandoning their moral qualms over Tiananmen, multinationals pressured the US state to grant China most-favored-nation status in 1993 and give it permanent normal trade relations in 2000. Other powers did the same, opening the floodgates for foreign capital to pour into the country to exploit its inexpensive land and low-cost labor. As a result, China's economy exploded from a mere 6 percent of US GDP in 1990 to 80 percent of it in 2012.[9] Multinational corporations spurred the boom. But China required foreign high-tech and capital-intensive corporations to transfer their technology to local state and private enterprises. Thus, the Chinese state supported the development of indigenous capital and enabled it to compete in the world system.

Deng's successors continued his economic strategy. During Jiang Zemin's rule from 1993 through 2002, the regime oversaw deeper free-market reforms—massive privatization of uncompetitive state-owned corporations, further relaxation of trade barriers and regulations, and the dismantling of social welfare provision. As a result of these privatization measures, employment in state industry was cut by tens of millions between 1997 and 2005.[10] And the state-owned sector's share of GDP dropped dramatically to now less than 30 percent.[11] In anticipation of even further free-market reforms, the US supported China's accession to the World Trade Organization in 2001. At the same time as Jiang accelerated China's opening to the global market, he was careful to maintain state ownership of key industries—the commanding heights of the national economy in core industries like transportation, energy, and finance. Through his "Go Out" policy, he encouraged state firms to secure ownership of, and shares in, foreign companies, especially in transportation, infrastructure, and natural resources, thereby deepening their integration into global capitalism. Thus, not only did China expand its receipt of FDI, it also became an international investor in its own right.

By the early 2000s, China's state and private capital were fully merged into the world economy. Its state corporations sold shares on stock markets from Hong Kong to New York, and they formed joint partnerships with multinationals. And its private corporations, which today account for more than 60 percent of China's GDP and 90 percent of its exports, expanded dramatically and forged partnerships with multinationals.[12] To accommodate these transformations, Jiang introduced his new "theory" about the role of the CCP—the "Three Represents"—that claims that the party represents the most advanced productive forces, advanced culture, and the interests of *all* Chinese people. The last was justification to openly allow membership in the party to private capitalists like Alibaba's billionaire owner, Jack Ma, who had actually held a party card since the 1980s.[13] While the party state's development strategy has reduced poverty on a massive scale, it has introduced new levels of class and social inequality. China's Gini coefficient, which measures income inequality, is on par with that of the US.[14] It now ranks just below the US as the country with the second-most billionaires, and their profits and wealth derive from the exploitation of the country's massive, poorly paid working class.[15]

CRISIS, STIMULUS, AND EXPANSION

China's integration into global capitalism and its crises challenged the state's ability to maintain control over its economy and society. Jiang's successor, Hu Jintao, who ruled the country from 2002 to 2012, tempered the market reforms, reemphasized the state sector, and increased subsidies to health care to ameliorate, at least in part, the country's growing class inequality. These growing disparities were a key factor in the rise in strikes and protests by workers and peasants, which skyrocketed in the 2000s and 2010s.[16] The bureaucracy's answer to such resistance was repression, co-optation, and a promise that further development would improve workers' standard of living.

The Great Recession that rocked the world system in 2008 threatened to undue such efforts. To get the economy growing again, Hu intensified the role of the state in the economy, implementing the largest stimulus program in the world, pouring $586 billion mainly into state corporations and infrastructure projects.[17] While this intensified its problems of debt, overcapacity, overproduction, and ecological devastation, it triggered another wave of expansion in China with growth skyrocketing back to 8.7 percent in 2009 and 10.4 percent in 2010.[18] Indeed, as the world economy cratered, China became the system's main growth engine, sustaining expansions in commodity exporting economies especially in Asia, Latin America, and Africa.

It used the so-called BRICS (Brazil, Russia, India, China, South Africa) alliance it forged in 2006 to posture as the leader of the developing world. But, in fact, China was reinforcing underdevelopment in countries in the Global South. In Latin America, its cheap exports have undercut the region's industries and reduced countries to shipping raw materials to China—the classic dependency trap. Brazil, for example, has experienced deindustrialization of major sectors of its economy in part because of its trade with China.[19] Its exports to China are almost entirely primary products, while its imports are manufactured goods.[20] The same is true with its trade partners in Africa like Angola, the Democratic Republic of the Congo, Egypt, Nigeria, South Africa, and Zambia. They export rare earth minerals, metals, and oil to China, and they import finished products. And China's development projects reinforce this pattern, building infrastructure and transportation systems designed to facilitate the extraction of commodities to fuel Beijing's economy—the classic imperialist pattern.[21]

RECLAIMING CHINA'S STATUS AS A GREAT POWER

China rode the long neoliberal boom from the early 1980s to the Great Recession to become a global economic power. In 2022, China had 136 companies (including state-owned and private) on the Fortune 500 list, just ahead of the US with 124 and far more than Japan's 47.[22] But rather than assert China's potential imperial power, Deng's successors followed his cautious foreign policy perspective that Beijing "observe calmly, secure our position, cope with affairs calmly, hide our capacities and bide our time, be good at maintaining a low profile and never claim leadership."[23] After his accession to power in 2012, Xi Jinping abandoned this approach to carry out what some call a "Third Revolution."[24] Xi announced a new foreign policy of "national rejuvenation" to achieve "The Chinese Dream" of reclaiming the country's status as a great power. His open assertion of Chinese imperial power has economic, geopolitical, and military dimensions.

On the economic front, he has reemphasized the importance of state-owned corporations, and the government continues to pour money into them through state banks. While that has strengthened the hand of the state in the economy, it has also exacerbated its problem of overinvestment and overcapacity. Xi's solution has been to export China's surplus capital and industrial capacity through the Belt and Road Initiative (BRI), which he announced in 2013. The plan calls for investment of over $1 trillion in infrastructure and transport spending in 150 countries, mainly in Europe, Asia, and Africa. It includes two main components—a "Silk Road Economic Belt" for overland transport routes linking Asia and Europe, connected to a "Maritime Silk Road" to establish ports for sea routes between Africa, Europe, the Middle East, and Asia.[25] This enormous project is, adjusted for inflation, seven times larger than the US Marshall Plan spent rebuilding Europe after World War Two.[26]

To fund this investment, China launched the New Development Bank in 2014 and the far more significant Asian Infrastructure Investment Bank in 2016. China boasts that its BRI loans do not have the same free-market conditionalities as those from the IMF (International Monetary Fund) and the World Bank, nor will they meddle with questions of corruption or human rights. But they are not without conditions, and the projects themselves are not done out of altruism toward the Global South, but to serve Chinese interests. The loans often require countries to contract China's state-owned corporations and hire Chinese labor.[27] And China has initiated all this development to export its excess manufacturing capacity, secure access to raw materials, and open new markets.[28] The projects also serve geopolitical aims. For example, China is helping Pakistan to build a port in Gwadar that would open overland trade routes that avoid bottlenecks like the Strait of Malacca between Malaysia and Indonesia, which is patrolled by the US Navy.[29]

Despite all the hype, BRI has run into numerous problems, from conflicts over the terms of investment to loan defaults, shoddy construction, exploitative labor conditions, and incomplete or suspended projects in various countries.[30] Moreover, the combination of the pandemic recession, increased inflation during the recovery, and interest rate hikes in advanced capitalist countries have triggered a new debt crisis throughout the Global South, including in countries on the receiving end of BRI loans from China. As a result, a growing list of countries have demanded renegotiation of their debts with Beijing. Such government resistance and even more threatening mass resistance from below could lead China to enforce its interests militarily. Indeed, terrorist attacks on Chinese people and infrastructure in Balochistan have already led to some in China calling for increased deployment of security forces in the region. All of this has taken the initial shine off BRI and led Xi to significantly curtail expenditures since 2016. But he remains committed to the project to secure China's central position in global capitalism.[31]

NATIONAL HIGH-TECH CHAMPIONS

Xi has also launched several economic initiatives to escape the classic middle-income trap of producing manufactured goods for the world system while remaining stuck at a low level of development and unable to compete at levels higher up the value chain. Xi's most important initiative to avoid this has been "Made in China 2025." The state has funded national champions in high tech like Huawei to compete with US, European, and Asian multinationals.[32] After a backlash from Western powers for its state support of such industries, China abandoned the phrase but still pursues the policy and practice.

Beijing is funding state and private corporations to upgrade their capacities in a whole range of industries that are part of what has been called a "Fourth Industrial Revolution."These include microchips, information technology, artificial intelligence, robotics, and green energy. This program has brought China into direct competition with the advanced capitalist countries in high value-added production. In some cases, China has managed to leapfrog its competitors, especially in 5G, which is central to the so-called "internet of things" that connects all sorts of devices, infrastructure, and wireless networks to each other over the internet.[33] The high-tech industry has applications for the military and especially forms of conflict like cyberwarfare. Thus, the US in particular has regarded China 2025 as a threat to its supremacy on both economic and military grounds. That's why Washington has called Huawei a national security threat and banned its 5G system, blocked sales of high-end microchips to it, and pressured other countries to do the same.[34]

The US and its allies can bully China and its companies because they have a near monopoly on research and development of high-end microchips and semiconductors. As the founder of the Taiwanese company TSMC (Taiwan Semiconductor Manufacturing Company), Morris Chang, boasted, "We control all the choke points. China can't really do anything if we want to choke them."[35] The US demonstrated this power when the Trump administration banned chip sales to ZTE over its supposed skirting of sanctions on Iran, nearly bankrupting the company overnight.[36] This attack spurred China to pour money into its indigenous chip and semiconductor industry to neutralize Washington's attempt to paralyze its companies with sanctions and trade barriers.

BOLSTERING THE PARTY STATE

Xi paired his reassertion of state capitalism with bolstering the CCP's rule over all aspects of Chinese society and a crackdown on resistance of any kind. He launched a campaign against corruption within the state, whose bureaucrats routinely use their positions for personal gain. The state has indicted over one hundred thousand officials for various crimes and probed a total of five million.[37] Xi also launched a far-reaching effort to discipline private corporations. He has placed CCP bureaucrats on most boards, blocked them from selling shares on foreign stock markets, disciplined corporate moguls for opposition to increased regulation, and demanded their allegiance to the state's priorities. This has impacted everything from Jack Ma's Ant Group and the ride-sharing corporation DiDi to private education companies like New Oriental.[38]

This crackdown on parts of the private sector has been paired with enhanced Chinese nationalism as part of the CCP's assertion of its status as a great power. That, along with the promise of improved standards of living, have been the principal means for the state to maintain its popular support and legitimacy. Xi has used this nationalism to justify the state's mass policing and detention of Uyghurs in Xinjiang, crushing of the uprising in Hong Kong, and denial of the right to self-determination in Tibet and Inner Mongolia. Unsurprisingly, this repression often dovetails with the state's economic interests, especially in Xinjiang with its extensive cotton industry and BRI projects.[39]

At the same time, Xi and the bureaucracy realize that they must rebalance the economy and address the deep inequality, land grabs, and environmental crises that have driven waves of protest over the last decade. He launched his "Common Prosperity" program to raise the standard of living and increase household consumption, which has dropped from just under 55 percent of GDP in 1985 to about 39 percent in 2019.[40] That would correct the overinvestment in production and infrastructure, but any increase in wages and benefits undermines the basis of China's boom—the country's cheap labor reserves. Thus, Xi's promise of increased standards of living for most workers has not produced meaningful results. Wage increases have stalled, minimum wages hikes have slowed, and social spending remains low. As with the 2008 crisis, the state's response to slowing growth during the pandemic lockdowns largely focused on assisting firms, not workers.[41]

Finally, Xi has tried to mitigate the profound environmental crises caused by China's capitalist industrialization. He has invested in green energy and at least some increased regulation on the worst polluters. Indeed, China has positioned itself as one of the global innovators and producers of green technology and infrastructure. But rather than address the environmental crisis, most of these measures have merely displaced the worst practices to underdeveloped regions within the country and abroad. The government's 2021 promise to end funding for overseas coal plants is a positive development, and activists should continue to hold BRI projects accountable for their ecological impact, wherever on the planet they are located. Such activism will be essential as Beijing, despite its promise, approved the construction of nearly two new coal plants a week inside China in 2022, building the most it has since 2015.[42]

FORGING ECONOMIC, POLITICAL, AND SECURITY ALLIANCES

While Xi consolidated state control at home, he has projected Beijing's power abroad, forging various economic, political, and security alliances. In Asia, he inked the Regional Comprehensive Economic Partnership, an enormous trade deal with the region's main economic powers. It includes Australia, Brunei, Cambodia, Indonesia, Japan, Laos, Malaysia, Myanmar, New Zealand, Singapore, South Korea, Thailand, and Vietnam. It cut over 90 percent of the tariffs in the region and established common rules for trade, e-commerce, and intellectual property rights. Importantly, it includes no prohibitions on state ownership and backing of corporations, in contrast to such pacts struck by the US. It also has no labor protections whatsoever.[43]

China is pursuing similar deals with other powers and regions of the world economy. For example, it is trying to seal a deal with the EU, the Comprehensive Agreement on Investment, that includes promises of market liberalization by both parties as well as an end to forced technology transfers. That China was willing to make such concessions is a sign of its increased strength and confidence. While it was agreed to in principle by the EU and China against the wishes of the US, which fears greater penetration of the European market by China, it faces stiff opposition in the European Parliament, where it has yet to win approval.

Finally, China has sought economic and security pacts with allies. It has placed increasing importance on its BRICS alliance as a potential economic bloc and counterweight to US-dominated formations like the G7. Its most important security alliance is the Shanghai Cooperation Organization, originally formed in 1996 with Kazakhstan, Kyrgyzstan, Russia, and Tajikistan. It expanded to include Uzbekistan, India, and Pakistan with observer status granted to Afghanistan, Belarus, Iran, and Mongolia. Through the alliance, China has established economic linkages throughout Eurasia, agreements on mutual security, and joint military exercises. Beijing and Russia have used the pact to shield themselves and other states against criticism of human rights violations from the US and other powers by coordinated voting for one another in the UN.

They have done so especially since the Arab Spring in 2011, which both China and Russia looked at as threatening examples of popular revolts against autocratic regimes. They characterized them as so-called color revolutions orchestrated by Washington, especially after the US-led NATO intervention in Libya against Muammar Gaddafi's dictatorship. Since then, China, Russia, and their allies have backed regimes against democratic uprisings in various countries, including Syria, Thailand, and Myanmar. Increasingly, an informal network of undemocratic regimes has come into being in opposition to the US and its allies. Now they routinely unite in UN votes against Washington. This has all come to a head in the wake of Russia's invasion of Ukraine with China tacitly supporting Moscow and excusing its barbarous war as a justified response to NATO enlargement.[44]

MILITARY MODERNIZATION

To back China's assertion of economic and geopolitical power, Xi has accelerated the modernization of its military. The government has increased military spending by between 6 and 7 percent each year, driving the budget up from $11.25 billion in 1989 to $293.35 billion in 2021, the second highest in the world. But China remains well behind the whopping $801 billion spent by the US in 2021.[45] Nevertheless, it has become a major military power. It has oriented its military spending on high-tech weaponry, cyberwarfare, nuclear missiles, and militarization of space, all with the aim of catching up with or neutralizing Washington's military dominance, especially in the Asia Pacific.

China has cashed in on this military development to become one of the world's largest arms traders. It now ranks fourth behind the US, Russia, and France.[46] It has shipped munitions to regimes in Asia, Africa, and the Middle East. Its largest market is in Pakistan. Xi's military buildup and weapons trade is entirely imperial in nature. The People's Liberation Army made this explicit in a 2013 white paper: "With the gradual integration of China's economy into the world economy system, overseas interests have become an integral component of China's national interests. Security issues are increasingly prominent, involving overseas energy and resources, strategic sea lines of communication, and Chinese nationals and legal persons overseas."[47]

To push back against the US presence in what China sees as its own sphere of influence in the Asian Pacific, Xi has adopted a military strategy of anti-access/area denial. China aims to deploy warships, fighter jets, and specialized missiles to neutralize Washington's advantages in bases and aircraft carriers. It has also pursued an aggressive program of establishing military bases on islands it claims in the South China Sea as well as territorial claims against various states in the East China Sea. The bases in the South China Sea enforce China's claims to fisheries and undersea energy reserves as well as protect its access to vital shipping lanes like the Strait of Malacca, which sees $5 trillion in trade pass through annually.[48]

This projection of power in the South and East China Seas has brought China into conflict with several Asian states, like Japan, the Philippines, Brunei, Taiwan, Vietnam, Indonesia, and Malaysia. It has also raised the ire of the US as well as Britain, and especially Australia. In a sign that its ambitions are not just regional, but global, China established its first overseas military base in Djibouti, on the Horn of Africa. It plans to add another one in Equatorial Guinea. Of course, these outposts pale in comparison to Washington's empire of bases. The US has an estimated eight hundred military installations all around the world that still enforce its status as the global superpower.[49]

THE CONTRADICTIONS AND FRAGILITY OF CHINESE IMPERIALISM

While China is a rising imperial power and rival to the US, its strength should not be exaggerated, nor its fragility underestimated. It has an abundance of political, economic, and military problems that it will not find easy to overcome. It is suffering slowing growth; increased indebtedness; overcapacity; ineffectual investment; corruption; an aging, shrinking, and increasingly expensive workforce, angered by the high levels of inequality, youth unemployment, and increased severity of various forms of oppression. These were compounded by the pandemic, lockdowns, and economic slowdown. The state's abandonment of its brutal zero-COVID-19 policy and its reopening will do little to overcome these underlying problems. Indeed, China's economy was slumping in 2023. These problems threaten China's continued rise and could trigger resistance from within, especially if its growth slows enough to threaten expectations of a better life in the future for the country's people.

Moreover, despite its rise, China remains dependent on advanced capitalist countries, especially the US. It needs them for markets as well as for inputs, especially the advanced microchips that it is not yet able to manufacture on its own. For all the talk of decoupling, global capitalism binds these imperial rivals together. Similarly, China's attempt to project its rising economic power has hit contradictions. Its Belt and Road Initiative became overextended, with too many projects that encountered a host of problems, forcing it to retreat. It did so not only because it wanted to avoid wasteful boondoggle projects, but also because it feared defaults and excessive capital flight from the national economy.

Similarly, it became cautious about its China 2025 program, which has triggered blowback from the US and others, forcing at least an initial rhetorical retreat. With the US escalation of restrictions of high tech, however, Xi has doubled down on funding high-tech national champions. These initiatives provoked opposition from states large and small to Beijing's assertion of itself as a new great power. Finally, China faces a profound environmental crisis.

Despite its professed intention to mitigate its emissions, it cannot do so and at the same time continue its economic ascent. Just like the US and European powers, China is now a culprit of climate change. These contradictions and fragilities, however, will not drive it to retreat from its assertion of itself as a great power. If anything, it will make it more determined to secure that status even if that project brings it into greater conflict with the system's hegemon, the US.

PART II

CLASS, SOCIAL, AND NATIONAL STRUGGLES IN CHINA

CHAPTER 3

CLASS STRUGGLE IN THE COUNTRYSIDE, CITIES, AND WORKPLACES

There is nothing magical about China's economic "miracle." China's growth is predicated on the exploitation of the working class, unpaid reproductive labor, especially of women, and dispossession of the people's land, natural resources, and collectively held assets. These forms of exploitation and theft benefit not only China's elites, but have helped ensure the profitability of capitalism at the *global* level, thereby enriching corporations and investors from the wealthy countries of North America, Europe, and Asia. If there is a secret to China's capitalist expansion, it is simply that the state has devised highly advanced governance strategies for ensuring rates of exploitation that are not possible elsewhere.

Nonetheless, the state's efforts to seamlessly incorporate China's workers and peasants into the circuits of global capitalist accumulation have been met with often fierce resistance. Peasants have consistently fought back against the corrupt and anti-democratic practices of land seizure and marketization. Their urban counterparts have done the same. People have organized against the razing of whole neighborhoods at the behest of land-greedy developers and their allies in city government. In the 1990s, workers mobilized against the theft of public assets during the privatization of state-owned firms. As the private sector came to play a larger role in China's employment landscape during the 2000s, the gravitational center of labor unrest increasingly shifted to private firms. Migrant workers from the countryside have taken up the mantle of resistance within the factories and in the rapidly expanding service sector.

Social unrest expanded dramatically over the 1990s and 2000s. "Mass incidents," as the government calls worker and peasant collective acts of more than twenty-five people, hit 87,000 in 2005, the year the government stopped reporting data. By 2010, prominent sociologist Sun Liping estimated that there were 180,000 mass incidents per year.[1] While overwhelming surveillance and repression have kept class struggles in China fractured and politically subordinated, such high levels of unrest demonstrate that the country's peasantry and working class are determined to fight to improve their conditions. Even without formal organization, these struggles have wrested major symbolic, legal, and material victories from the state and capital alike. Any hope for economic justice and social liberation in China rests largely on the future dynamics of these movements.

CHINA'S LAND OWNERSHIP SYSTEM

Land and land rights have been key sites of resistance. China's land tenure system and changes to it form the basis of rural class struggle. Following the revolution, most land in China was given either a rural or urban designation. In the 1940s and 1950s, land in rural areas was distributed to family units, and then later collectivized at the level of the village. In the lead up to the Great Leap Forward in the late 1950s, many village collectives were amalgamated into communes with the aim of increasing productivity. The failures of the Great Leap are well-known, and many millions of people starved to death largely as a result of the state's exploitative policies in the countryside. After Mao's death, Deng Xiaoping pioneered market reform in the countryside. While the village collective maintained ownership, land use rights were returned to family units. Critically, ownership decisions were, and still are, supposed to be made by all people who have household registration within the collective. Indeed, land rights are the one benefit that rural people maintain that urban residents do not have.

While urban residents enjoy far superior access to social services, they cannot own land. In fact, most land in cities is owned by local governments, which use this power to overcome their limited ability to levy taxes (including property taxes) and raise revenue. They evict masses of people from land and buildings and auction off long-term leases to developers, who then build privately owned buildings on the land. Thus, government ownership of the land has not blocked but in fact facilitated the development of a capitalist market in housing and commercial real estate.[2] These differing patterns of land tenure as well as the uneven development of capitalism have resulted in unique dynamics of land-based class struggle in the countryside and city.

The central problem that rural residents face is that they often have no meaningful channels to exercise their nominal collective right to control the land. Government officials violate that right and make unilateral decisions about how to dispose of land with little to no public oversight. Officials simply invoke eminent domain, expropriate land, and make deals with private developers, often at far below the "market rate"—a process that is unsurprisingly rife with corruption. Officials are only required to compensate villagers for the agricultural value of the land, regardless of what kind of use the land will be put to after development. As a result, land compensation is, as a rule, woefully inadequate.

A comprehensive study by Landesa found that farmers generally were paid just over 2 percent of the amount that village authorities made from contracts with developers.[3] Given this brazen theft of collective property, it is hardly surprising that the same survey found that people were dissatisfied with land takings by a two-to-one margin. In the context of China's rapid industrialization, urbanization, and infrastructure expansion, land expropriation has hardly been a marginal phenomenon. One study estimates that 130 million people lost their land between 1991 and 2013.[4] Thus, the creation of gargantuan real estate, construction, and transportation companies—central pillars of Chinese capitalism—has been underwritten by mass evictions and dispossession of rural land.

RURAL STRUGGLES AGAINST DISPOSSESSION

Rural people have staged frequent and spectacular protests against this vast enclosure of supposedly collectively held land. In contrast to many others around the world, rural people in China typically do not refuse to leave the land and do not express a deep cultural commitment to agrarian life. Rather, in a society where "development" is a hegemonic idea, their main demand is adequate compensation to avoid severe poverty after eviction. People with rural *hukou* are excluded from urban social services, and rural services are far inferior. Their access to land is the key to their economic security and means of social reproduction. As a result, when evicted without fair payment for the loss of their access to land, they face poverty without any real social welfare safety net to ease their conditions. Unsurprisingly, fear of this fate has motivated rural people to stage some of the most intense and even violent social struggles in recent memory.

Perhaps the best-known land struggle of the last couple of decades took place in 2011 in eastern Guangdong's Wukan. Over many years, the village leadership had sold land use rights to various private interests to build industrial and commercial properties. While officials had raked in tens of millions of dollars, villagers were granted a pittance of the rents, violating the stipulation that profits from collectively held land are supposed to be shared among all members of the community. This blatant inequity generated outrage among the villagers. For years they organized and petitioned the government to right this wrong, but to no avail.

In 2011, villagers frustrated with government inaction began organizing public demonstrations and fighting riot cops sent to suppress them. When a healthy middle-aged man died in police custody, villagers became incensed, chased the government officials and police out of town, and established their direct control over the area. The government then laid siege to the village and a tense standoff ensued over many days. The protesters demanded adequate compensation for their land, the removal of corrupt officials, and, most strikingly, the right to democratically elect their village leadership. Provincial-level officials intervened and negotiated a settlement, promising to provide better compensation and to schedule an election. Although villagers would come to be quite frustrated by the political process in the years to follow, the state's willingness to compromise, rather than resort to pure repression, was a significant victory.

The protests in Wukan were exceptional in terms of the level of sustained mobilization, as well as the huge amount of media attention it garnered. But it revealed several issues that are widespread. First, mass expropriation is a direct outgrowth of the absence of democratic control over land. As one of the key organizers of the protest put it, "As a villager of Wukan, my original aim was to regain the land that had been stolen and sold by the government. Of course, this touches on issues of democracy: the lack of democracy means that village affairs are not transparent. This is one of the reasons that the land could be stolen and sold behind the villagers' backs."[5] These conditions more or less hold in every village in China.

Second, the resistance also shows how even as more people migrate to the cities for waged employment, they regard access to land (and the rents it can generate) as essential for ensuring their subsistence. Given the low wages they are paid in the cities, migrant workers require other forms of livelihood like land rent. Finally, and most optimistically, the Wukan uprising demonstrates the ongoing potential for rural people to radicalize and exert their collective power in reaction to threats of dispossession. Indeed, in response to persistent unrest from the 1990s on, the government has taken steps to reign in some of the most exploitative practices of land expropriation.

THE STRUGGLE FOR THE CITY

Political dynamics for urban residents, who have rights to urban social services but none over land use, have been different, despite some shared grievances. Chinese cities have been dramatically remade over the past generation, as the country's urban population rate shot from 19 percent in 1980 to 65 percent in 2022.[6] The character of cities has changed in the process. In the Mao era, the state focused on the development of urban industry. Today, state and capital have concentrated on real estate development, IT, the service sector, and retail markets for consumers. That reorientation has required massive displacement and relocation of urban residents. The phrase *chaiqian*—demolition and relocation—came to symbolize the experience of tens of millions of people in cities in the early twenty-first century. Nevertheless, most have accepted such redevelopment and gentrification as a necessary part of economic growth and so rarely oppose such projects altogether. Instead, they have waged struggles for just compensation.

City officials and developers have colluded in the transformation of China's cities, enriching themselves in the process. Many of the country's billionaires have made their money in real estate, redevelopment, and gentrification. In cities like Beijing and Shanghai, these moguls do not invest in changing cities building by building; they wipe out entire neighborhoods all at once, clearing the way for massive luxury apartment blocks, high-rise business districts, glitzy "mixed-used" complexes and malls that overshadow their US counterparts. It takes immense political courage as well as serious organization to try to stand in the way of such overbearing political and economic power.

As the phrase *chaiqian* suggests, urban residents struggle not only for compensation for lost property, but also over the terms of relocation. Compensation is often a tricky issue as former residents of the urban core sometimes had property rights to their housing, and sometimes did not. The state has almost never provided people with market rates for their property. So, given that they accept redevelopment, they have mainly fought over where they will be relocated and the size, quality, and price of the new housing. Typically, city governments relocate people to apartments in new suburban high-rise complexes. When done right, this may be an upgrade since much Mao-era housing was cramped and of poor quality, often with subpar heating, and with multiple families sharing limited bathroom and kitchen facilities. Owning a modern, air-conditioned, and sunny apartment can hold a lot of appeal—especially if the government subsidizes the purchase price enough and it is in an area with increasing property values.

Of course, relocation often does not work out so well. And, as with their rural counterparts, urban residents have sometimes been able to mobilize collectively to defend themselves. This rarely prevents the relocations altogether, but can win them better compensation, or a better apartment out in the suburbs. In some highly publicized cases, such resistance has produced "nail houses"— tenants who refuse the terms of relocation and hold on to their residence even as the site around them is demolished. The central government has become sensitive to protests by urban residents and has pressured cities to take a slower and more consultative approach to redevelopment, while also setting standards for better compensation.

Only residents with urban household registrations have been able to strike better deals for compensation and relocation. Migrant workers in cities have not been granted any improvement in their rights. Although nonlocals represent a large share of the population of all major cities, ranging from one-third to more than half of the total urban population, their rights are ignored as they are treated as disposable in the process of urban redevelopment. Working-class migrants often reside in informal housing and are therefore entitled to no compensation or relocation accommodations in the event of demolitions. The same holds true for the informal schools that migrant children attend. These rarely have official licensing and can be subjected to arbitrary closure or demolition with no accommodation made for the students.

Demolitions of migrant housing and schools have often spurred intense resistance. This has included blockading of roads and bulldozers, public protests at government agencies, and even self-immolations. While these have occasionally wrested victories in delaying demolition or securing a modicum of compensation, non-local residents in cities continue to be treated as expendable. When urban officials judge the value of the land under migrant homes and schools to exceed the value of their labor, they are quick to expel them.

RESISTING THE RESTRUCTURING OF STATE-OWNED ENTERPRISES

Parallel and often in tandem with these rural and urban struggles over land and housing, workers have staged waves of resistance at the point of production in China's vast new industries. To understand the character of this struggle, it is important to grasp the transformation of China's labor market. Despite their relative material security and relatively high social status, workers in SOEs were subject to antidemocratic practices by enterprise bureaucrats as well as pressure to meet increased production targets. Grievances over these conditions sparked collective action, most spectacularly represented by the massive 1957 strike wave in Shanghai. Later, during the Cultural Revolution, insurgent workers allied with rebel students to air their grievances against overbearing enterprise bureaucrats and useless company unions, and workers played a major role in social upheavals in many cities throughout China.

Deng's market reforms dramatically changed the conditions of work and character of struggle. Over time, they reduced the role of SOEs to roughly one-quarter of China's GDP and subjected them to market forces.[7] SOE bureaucrats gained the authority to hire and fire workers while their industries lost their "soft budget" and were forced to compete with rivals, including in the private sector. To stay afloat, the SOEs laid off workers and cut the wages and benefits of those who remained. While China avoided Russian-style shock therapy, which dismantled almost all state-owned industry, it did carry out massive restructuring of the state sector, beginning in 1997. Tens of millions of workers lost their jobs, and those who did retain them were subject to productivity squeezes as what had remained of the "iron rice bowl" was dismantled.

Workers resisted these market reforms with waves of struggle. From the late 1990s through the late 2000s, they staged protests and strikes against layoffs, pension thefts, and privatization. Perhaps the most famous example was the movement in Liaoyang in 2002, when tens of thousands of SOE workers rose up against factory closures, threatening social stability. Many other protests employed radical tactics like road and rail blockades. In 2009, workers at Tonghua Iron and Steel Group in Jilin province captured and beat to death an executive from the private company that was leading a privatization effort. The state responded with repression, arresting and sentencing leaders to long prison sentences. Workers who lost their jobs found themselves in the private labor market without much hope of finding decent work. Nevertheless, their fierce resistance contributed to Hu Jintao's decision to back off further privatization of state industry.

MIGRANT CLASS STRUGGLE IN CHINA'S NEW INDUSTRIES

By the beginning of the twenty-first century, these struggles by SOE workers were increasingly overshadowed by those of migrant workers in the private sector. Unlike the old industrial workers in the state sector, these workers have very little job security, poor to nonexistent social insurance coverage, and almost entirely depend on wages for their social reproduction. Migrants from the countryside are second-class workers in the stratified internal citizenship regime. They are excluded from social services in their adopted cities because their household registration, their *hukou*, is tied to their rural towns. On the one hand, their access to benefits there does provide them with some buffer during spells of unemployment. But, on the other hand, their precarious status in the cities makes them a super-exploitable workforce for both Chinese and multinational industries.

One thing that has *not* changed since Deng's market reforms is the system of working-class representation, which is still monopolized by the All-China Federation of Trade Unions (ACFTU). While it claims to be a union, it is in fact an arm of the state, and serves most importantly to ensure a quiescent workforce. The bureaucrats at the top of the AFCTU hold positions in the government. Independent mass labor organizations are simply not tolerated. This state monopoly on union representation combined with the stratified internal citizenship regime—both inherited from the Mao era—have been key to creating a cheap and politically repressed working-class numbering in the hundreds of millions.

It was precisely this workforce that the state identified as its comparative advantage as the country became integrated into global capitalism. The flood of investment that came to China from the 1990s on was initially concentrated in labor-intensive manufacturing where workers could expect deplorable conditions. These workers responded to their exploitation with militant labor struggles, just like working classes in other countries that have undergone similar processes of industrialization. Their demands centered on wages, conditions, and legal protections. While the government provides no official statistics, it is clear that strikes and protests increased dramatically from the 1990s to the mid-2010s, averaging thousands of mass incidents a year.

In the early years of market reform, much of the resistance was reactive and mainly focused on unpaid wages, egregious violations of workplace safety, and dignity on the job. Without union representation, workers relied on informal networks, often from their villages, to organize actions. Wildcat strikes became commonplace in special economic zones and manufacturing hubs like Shenzhen, Dongguan, and Guangzhou in South China. Most lasted only a few hours or a couple of days and often secured some concessions from management. This pattern continued as foreign investors built new factories and employed ever-greater numbers of migrant workers.

Over the course of the 2000s and early 2010s, workers built more sophisticated organizations and used a greater variety of tactics, often assisted by the developing network of labor NGOs. These were supported by activists in Hong Kong and grew in number to support the ever-growing needs of migrant workers in China's booming economy. A small number of labor NGOs adopted a more militant approach, shifting their focus from legal aid to helping workers organize networks of militant activists. While their number remained small and influence limited by their nonmembership structure, the labor NGOs played an outsized role in amplifying worker mobilizations. However, the vast majority of worker mobilizations remained autonomous.

In an attempt to quell this wave of militancy, the Chinese government enacted labor reforms that codified basic workers' rights. The ACFTU was also driven to experiment with limited reforms to better represent workers' interests in managing labor conflict. Yet this did not succeed in tamping down strikes or protests and may have actually inspired workers by rewarding their actions and giving them legal legitimacy. The tightening labor market also gave them confidence to advance their struggle, a dynamic particularly apparent in the industrial heartland of Guangdong.

Workers went on the offensive, demanding wage increases above the legal requirements. A strike at the Honda Nanhai transmission plant triggered a massive strike wave in the auto industry in the summer of 2010. In 2014, forty thousand workers took action at the Taiwanese-owned Yue Yuen shoe factory, signaling workers' increased organizational capacity, something aided in no small part by local NGOs. Such struggle was not restricted to the manufacturing sector. Schoolteachers, taxi drivers, sanitation workers, Walmart retail store workers, construction workers, and many others organized actions at their workplaces during the same period. Most of these were led and made up of migrant workers. Together they posed a serious challenge to the government as well as Chinese and multinational corporations.

LABOR STRUGGLES AFTER THE GREAT RECESSION

In retrospect, the mid-2010s marked the high-water mark for migrant workers' struggle, as a variety of factors have since compromised their strength. The 2008 economic crisis undermined labor-intensive manufacturing, which had been the epicenter of this wave of unrest. Tens of millions of migrant workers employed in China's export-processing sector lost their jobs as factories shut their doors. The state responded to the crisis with a massive economic stimulus program; it opened the spigot of government credit to finance an unprecedented investment in infrastructure and real estate. While that enabled China to avoid slipping into the recession that swept the US and Europe, it could not sustain the decade-long annual growth rate of 10 percent and the investment-led growth created new problems for Chinese capitalism, most importantly overcapacity and indebtedness.

At the same time, the combination of workers' struggle and the shrinking pool of young workers increased the cost of labor, encouraging companies to begin relocating labor-intensive and wage-sensitive industries like textile manufacturing to countries in Southeast and South Asia. As a result, manufacturing's significance for both employment and economic growth peaked, plateaued, and in some cases declined. Some export-oriented regions of the country such as the Pearl River Delta have already experienced *dein*dustrialization, along with attendant labor struggles against layoffs and for compensation for lost jobs. All these changes negatively impacted workers' ability to organize on the job.

This also forced China to attempt adjustments in its development strategy. The state tried to decrease Chinese capitalism's dependence on export industries and foreign consumers by spurring domestic investment. The state has been aggressive in its effort to climb up the value chain to make its companies globally competitive. This has entailed more capital-intensive forms of manufacturing, which have in general required fewer workers with higher levels of education. This has reduced employment opportunities at the lower end of the labor market.

At the same time, capital has increasingly built up the service sector, especially the gig economy. This created new conditions for labor organizing. While there have been small-scale strikes among gig workers and those in the service sector, they have not been on the same scale, nor have they had the same dramatic political effect as strikes in manufacturing. By the end of the second decade of the twenty-first century, the Chinese working class was (numerically at least) concentrated in the service sector.

Thus, structural changes in the economy dissipated the wave of struggle. The state also contributed to this demobilization, using political repression to dampen working-class resistance. This was relatively easy due to the lack of strong organization among workers. Despite the waves of militancy from the 2000s through the early 2010s, the actions were localized and ephemeral, making it very difficult for militants to build formal workplace and political organizations. The state did all it could to prevent such organizations from developing. In late 2015, it cracked down on labor NGOs, depriving workers in the industrial centers of a critical source of knowledge, advice, and support. The NGOs that have survived can only do so by restricting themselves to providing services.

Similarly, the state disrupted support for labor struggles in universities. It shuttered labor studies centers, fired pro-labor faculty, and harassed and surveilled student activists. The 2018 efforts by Marxist student groups to support the struggle of Jasic workers in Shenzhen represented the boldest and most explicitly political effort to build student-worker solidarity since 1989.[8] But despite, or perhaps *because* of, the students' professed allegiance to Marxism and Maoism, the state responded with astonishing severity, disappearing several activists, arresting and charging others, and subjecting dozens, if not hundreds, of students to threats, repression, and surveillance. Since 2018 it has been almost impossible for activists to engage in any sustained labor campaigns.

But no one should mistake this lull in struggle as somehow diminishing the Chinese working class's objective power or subjective willingness to fight. In the fall of 2022, it once again demonstrated its militancy in opposition to the government's increasingly repressive pandemic controls. These had taken a huge toll on workers, millions of whom had been deprived of basic livelihood during long-term lockdowns in their homes. In other cases, companies imposed "closed-loop" work arrangements that forced workers to remain in their workplaces, denying them the right to go home. So, they worked, ate, and slept in their factories. These policies generated a wave of small-scale protests and riots over the spring and summer of 2022, including at Apple's supplier Quanta and in numerous working-class neighborhoods throughout the country.

In October 2022, this wave crested at Zhengzhou's Foxconn factory complex, the world's largest iPhone manufacturer, which accounts for three-quarters of global output of the iconic phone. To keep churning out products, Foxconn imposed closed-loop management, locking two hundred thousand workers inside its facility, denying them the right to leave even when the virus began to circulate among workers. The company failed to provide adequate food to workers, trapped the healthy and the sick together, and denied adequate care to those who contracted the illness. Fearful for their well-being, thousands of workers broke out of the complex, jumping over walls and rushing past security guards. With production paralyzed, Foxconn announced big bonuses to lure people back to work. Local officials in nearby villages helped with recruitment, going so far as to pressure military veterans to get production back up and running.

Foxconn, however, reneged on their offer and announced they would not be paying returned workers and new recruits their expected bonuses for many months. Outraged, workers staged perhaps the largest revolt in a decade, with thousands engaging in fierce physical battles with security guards, "big white" pandemic control workers, and the police. In the aftermath, Foxconn promised to pay 10,000 yuan to workers to *leave*—a huge victory for the rioters. But of greater political significance, this revolt initiated a sequence of resistance that would soon spread nationwide. The "White Paper Revolution"—so named for the blank sheets of paper protesters held—was the most politically significant social mobilization in China since 1989, and it was a movement catalyzed by workers.

CHINA'S CLASS STRUGGLES AND GLOBAL CAPITALISM

China's peasants and workers have waged heroic struggles in the face of the commodification of their land and labor. Again and again, they have challenged not only companies but also the Chinese state, which has lined up with SOEs and private corporations to steal land, raze established neighborhoods, and break strikes. The state has played an essential role in maintaining Chinese workers as a cheap, union-free workforce not only for domestic corporations but also multinationals from Apple and Walmart to Amazon and Tesla.

While these workers have not yet been able to sustain their own independent unions, let alone political formations, their struggle inevitably challenges the supply chains of global capitalism and the states that oversee them. For instance, when the Foxconn workers in Zhengzhou engaged in mass refusal of work in the fall of 2022, it caused heart palpitations in boardrooms from Taipei to Cupertino, demonstrating the power of the Chinese working class. Undoubtedly, Xi Jinping's repressive turn undercut the last wave of struggle, but it is clear that resistance continues to bubble beneath the surface and will inevitably explode in the coming years. The task for the international left is to recognize the deep connections among workers bound together in global production and distribution chains and lay the symbolic and organizational groundwork for more robust forms of solidarity and common struggle against our common enemies—the capitalist classes and their states from Washington to Beijing.

CHAPTER 4

FEMINIST RESISTANCE AND THE CRISIS OF SOCIAL REPRODUCTION

C hina's capitalist development has led to crises in people's lives that have not only produced waves of class struggle, but also precipitated movements against gender-based oppression. The new feminist movement is a response to a general crisis of social reproduction, of how the system births, rears, clothes, houses, and educates a new generation of workers. The crisis has intensified the oppression of women, who bear the double burden of both working and doing the bulk of unpaid and low-paid labor of social reproduction. Contemporary feminist movements in China attempt to challenge long-existing sexism that has been exacerbated by the deepening crisis of social reproduction. This struggle is part of the wave of feminist resistance globally that has involved everything from strikes by women workers to feminist strikes for political demands and struggles for reproductive justice around the world.

THE ROOTS OF CHINA'S CRISIS OF SOCIAL REPRODUCTION

In the pre-Reform era from 1949 to 1978, China established a two-tier system of social reproduction. In the urban first tier, state-owned enterprises (SOEs) provided their employees with housing, health care, schools, and services such as childcare and eldercare. In the rural second tier, state welfare provisions were much less elaborate, but the expansion of basic medical care and primary education significantly increased literacy and life expectancy. In the wake of market reforms, Chinese capitalism followed the global neoliberal trend of privatizing important aspects of social reproduction that radically altered both systems of social provisioning.

In the cities, the state privatized the majority of SOEs, laid off tens of millions of workers, and dismantled the welfare system tied to those workplaces. Militant resistance by SOE workers forced local governments to preserve some of the welfare benefits like pension schemes and health insurance. But even then, most services, including childcare, were privatized and turned into commodities purchased at high prices on the market. In the countryside, systematic underfunding of services, poverty, and lack of local opportunity drove rural workers and peasants to become migrant workers in the cities. In doing so, they gave up basic but guaranteed access to social welfare services, which were tied to their rural *hukou*, and they were largely denied such services in their adopted cities. The state thus turned these migrant workers into second-class citizens and cheap labor to be exploited by domestic and multinational corporations.

This restricted and largely privatized system of labor reproduction is now in crisis. In the cities, while the state maintained basic pensions and health care schemes, it privatized most other systems of social reproduction and forced households either to pay for them or rely on unpaid labor in the home or hire workers to carry them out. Today, China is among the very few countries in the world where there is zero government expenditure on care services for children under three. Public social spending as a share of GDP is shockingly low in China: in 2016 it was less than half that of the United States and Brazil, and less than one-third the levels of countries such as Germany or Norway.[1] Unsurprisingly, the price of childcare and other privatized necessities like housing, medicine, and education have skyrocketed. This new market has created a vast number of paid domestic women workers that do reproductive labor. Today, it is estimated that there are thirty-five million of these workers in China, making up the world's largest domestic service market.[2]

The state's commitment since the early 2010s to increase urbanization has intensified this crisis of social reproduction. In the last decade, the urban portion of the population increased from 53 percent in 2012 to 65 percent in 2022.[3] More than twenty million peasants have relinquished their land, which used to be both a means of making a living and, through their *hukou*, the means to access state social services, to become low-wage migrant wage laborers without access to any social services. This rapidly growing urban population has placed a rising demand on the inadequate supply of public services, forcing more and more people to turn to private education, health care, and domestic care. In turn these services have only grown more and more expensive.

The spiraling cost of privatized social reproduction has made it extremely difficult for families to afford the cost of bearing children, let alone rearing, caring for, and educating them. Even in the rural areas, private business has already made inroads not only in agricultural production but in social services as well. In fact, the migration of rural laborers from their households to the cities has made it impossible for them to provide care in the home for children and the elderly. Predictably, expensive private childcare and eldercare centers have filled the social void.

The high cost of social reproduction drives people to delay marriage and having children, resulting in progressively declining fertility rates. The number of marriage registrations has declined from an all-time high of 13.47 million in 2013 to 8.13 million in 2020, while divorce rates have surged to 3.37 million, seven times higher than it was three decades ago.[4] Until 2023, it was illegal for unmarried individuals to have children in China—making the low rate of marriage a major factor driving down fertility.[5] And when families do have children, they do not have many because of the cost of raising them. Accompanying the decline of fertility is the leveling off of demographic growth and population aging. According to China's seventh census released in May 2021, the country has a population of 1.41 billion, up by only 5.4 percent from a decade ago, and in 2022 the population decreased for the first time since the Great Famine in 1960.

THE STATE AND CAPITAL RESPOND TO THE CRISIS

The social reproduction crisis has led to a consensus among economists, demographers, media pundits, and policymakers that China is facing, at a minimum, major demographic headwinds. These are, of course, real problems for Chinese capitalism, and the state is trying to implement policies to boost population growth. In response to the crisis, the Chinese state overturned the one-child policy in 2015, adopted a new two-child policy, and has now gone even further, imposing policies to encourage an even higher birth rate and population growth. These policies include encouraging early marriage, making divorce inconvenient by adding a "cooling off" period,[6] beginning to restrict abortion for "non-medical purposes,"[7] and providing compensation for each new birth. As Xi himself puts it, every Chinese "should promote filial piety and family harmony," it is women's task to "strike a balance between family and work" and to "take up social responsibilities while contributing to their families."[8]

This so-called demographic crisis has to be put in perspective. It is true that the population is aging faster than other countries at the same level of development. In other words, China is "getting older before it gets rich." Yet, the real problem from the state's viewpoint is not having fewer people in absolute numbers, but the decline of a relatively cheap and young labor force, which has up until now fueled the spectacular rise of China's economy. As of today, more than 50 percent of all Chinese migrant workers are older than forty, while just a decade ago, only 16 percent were older than forty. Thus, the state, its policymakers, and most commentators frame the problem as a purely demographic one and argue that the solution is to raise the retirement age and, ultimately, boost birth rates. In reality, this analysis ignores the underlying crisis of social reproduction that cannot be solved by such state imposed social engineering.

Whether by restricting births in the past or pushing to increase the fertility rate today, the Chinese state's unmistakable intent has been to limit women's reproductive autonomy. Of course, this turn is not particular to China, rather it is a common feature of many states variously under neoliberal, conservative, or authoritarian parties. In China, the state has not gone so far as to limit access to birth control, which is still widely available (ironically, thanks to the earlier one-child policy). But it has begun to implement a series of measures that it believes can help boost fertility rates, such as freeing unmarried people to legally have children, paying families a modest children's allowance (still only a drop in the bucket of the cost of raising children), and imposing restrictions on what it calls "non-medical abortions," a vague category that will give the state wide latitude to restrict reproductive rights in the coming years. However, it is unlikely that any of these measures will increase the fertility rate and the overall population because they fail to address the underlying crisis of social reproduction that is closely tied to class politics and gender justice. As recent statistics prove,[9] people are not going to have more children when it costs so much to raise them and when most social services are privatized or carried out by already overburdened working-class women and families.

Unsurprisingly, the state's pronatalist turn in population policy has intensified the oppression of LGBTQ communities, which had already been struggling amid general crackdowns on civic organizations.[10] Now, the state sees queer activism and media representation of queer people as a threat to their campaign to pressure people into heterosexual marriage and procreation, in order to provide capital with a new generation of workers. Such homophobia, again, is not unique to China but part of an international phenomenon of the right trumpeting family values and demonizing LGBTQ people.

THE IMPACT OF THE SOCIAL REPRODUCTIVE CRISIS ON WOMEN

While the bureaucracy's policies are ineffective in meeting their stated goal of increasing the fertility rate, they are deepening women's oppression in China. They impose heterosexist, patriarchal family norms, restrict women's bodily autonomy, and increase the double burden of women working and doing a disproportionate amount of paid and unpaid social reproductive labor. But this increased oppression is not experienced uniformly by all Chinese women.

Rural families, migrant workers, and women in particular, have disproportionately borne the brunt of the crisis of social reproduction. With parents working in the city and public care facilities underdeveloped, children and aging grandparents left behind in the villages suffer from a wide range of issues, from malnutrition to negligence, abuse, psychological stress, and crime. Children who are brought by their parents to the cities are denied access to the city public school systems and other urban welfare services, which are reserved for those with urban residency.[11] As a result, migrant children often only have access to education in privatized, unregulated schools. In fact, some migrant children in cities receive less public and familial support compared to their rural counterparts, who at least can go to local schools, albeit of lower quality than urban ones.

Migrant women workers are put in a terrible bind in the cities. Many find jobs in domestic care, which has become one of the largest sectors employing migrant women. They become caregivers for other people's children and elderly family members, while leaving their own children and aging parents uncared for, at home or in their rural villages. The businesses they work for are extremely lucrative. But domestic workers are not considered formal workers and are thus not protected by the labor law. So, without formal contracts, they can be terminated at any time. If they suffer any injury or harassment, they have no labor protections and can only file civil court cases, something quite expensive and out of reach for most workers.

For urban workers and their families, women again disproportionately suffer the consequences of the social reproduction crisis.
Most urban families have their health care, pension, and K-12 education covered by government-assisted programs and institutions,
but these are basic and sometimes inadequate. As a result, all sorts
of for-profit businesses have developed to offer services that workers
have to pay for out of pocket. For-profit childcare and eldercare
companies are typical examples, and they are expanding quickly.
Families have no choice but to spend inordinate amounts of money
on these services, eating into their incomes.

Urban middle-class households experience their own version
of the reproductive crisis. Faced with fierce competition in professional labor markets, these families engage in intensive parenting
and invest in tutoring and private lessons beyond public education
to give their children an advantage over their peers. Although the
government took the extreme measure of banning private tutoring companies in 2021, there is significant evidence that well-off
families have continued similar practices in different forms. Unsurprisingly, given the conventional gender norms in most families,
wives, mothers, and grandmothers perform more emotional and
cognitive labor in the family. In other words, while middle-class
families have outsourced a large number of domestic chores to paid
helpers, women in such families still spend many more hours doing
care work than their male counterparts. Under family and state
pressure, women in professional, middle-class families sometimes
give up their paid work to carry out and oversee all this social reproductive labor, leading in recent years to a significant decline in
female labor force participation.

These conditions have allowed employers to lower pay for
women. Pay for urban women relative to men dropped from 78
percent in 1990 to 67 percent in 2010, while for their rural counterparts this ratio dropped even more, from 79 percent to 60 percent over the same time period.[12] The government's adoption of its
pronatalist policy has only intensified this downward pressure on
women's salaries and wages. Increasingly, employers view women
as potential child bearers instead of workers. Women are blatantly

discriminated against in the workplace, as they receive lower wages and are disproportionately subjected to layoffs during economic downturns. Thus, women in both the working class and middle class are caught in the contradictions of China's social reproduction crisis. The state and capital need them to have more babies while at the same time exploiting their labor on the job. Chinese women are intensely oppressed by this classic double burden of exploitation as workers and oppression as biological and social reproducers of the labor force.

The privatization of social reproduction also oppresses children, particularly in the working class. Migrant children are often denied access to basic education. Most working-class families cannot afford full-time caregivers at home, elite kindergartens, schools, and expensive extracurricular classes. As a result, these children and young adults see increasingly dim chances for upward mobility. Middle-class youth despair at the cutthroat environment they are being groomed for. This widespread frustration among working- and middle-class youth has been represented in often sensationalist stories in the domestic and international media about migrant drifters who decide to "work for a day, party for three" or "lying-flat" urbanites who give up on career competition and even refuse to marry and reproduce.[13]

CHINA'S NEW FEMINIST MOVEMENTS

While China and the Global North share many features of the neoliberal crisis of social reproduction, China has its own distinct historical and political-economic characteristics. China implemented state-sponsored "women's liberation" under the banner of "socialism" in the mid-twentieth century and carried out a particular form of state intervention in social reproduction. Understanding what this state-organized gender leveling did and did not achieve is a key to understanding the emergence of today's Chinese feminist movements.

Despite many limitations, the Chinese state had mitigated traditional patriarchal structures, brought women into the public sphere, and decreased economic, political, and social inequalities between men and women. Contrary to the conventional understanding, these achievements were not freely given by male leaders but fought for by revolutionary feminists working within the party system.[14] One institutional legacy of their efforts is the All-China Women's Federation (ACWF), which in the first decades of the PRC helped implement a set of progressive policies including equal pay, free marriage, paid maternity leave, public childcare, and other benefits. Ironically, today, that same organization is now helping propagate Xi's conservative agenda to cultivate "traditional family values." In other words, the ACWF has been turned on its head; it has abandoned its stated commitment to women's liberation and embraced a new role as the state's handmaiden in enforcing women's oppression.

The state's market reforms, consequent crisis of social reproduction, and Xi's new pronatalist policies have precipitated the rise of a new women's movement. It has taken different forms over the last few decades. In the late 1980s, and particularly after the Beijing World Conference on Women in 1995, feminist NGOs emerged to advocate for women's rights, address growing gender inequality, and combat gender-based violence. While representing women across all social classes, these NGOs were usually run by feminists from the professional and academic sectors and financed by international funding agencies. Around 2010, as international funding dried up and the state began to crack down on all NGOs, these new feminist institutions either closed or were shut down.[15]

In their absence, a new generation of Chinese women has begun to organize in different and more radical ways. A group of college students and young professionals from both urban and rural backgrounds built a new formation, Youth Feminist Activism. They have campaigned, protested, fought legal cases, set up social media platforms, performed plays, and staged walkathons, all calling for reforms to address gender discrimination and violence throughout

society. When the state arrested five of the group's most prominent figures in 2015, they were forced to become decentralized and
adopt new tactics. This strategic reorientation did not necessarily
mean the movement became weaker. Quite the opposite: the Chinese #MeToo movement, which started with a single complaint online in 2018, swept the internet, and compiled a thousand-page file
documenting cases of sexual harassment and rape.[16]

In the same year, a Chinese student at the University of Min-
nesota, Liu Jingyao, filed a lawsuit against Chinese tech billionaire Liu Qiangdong, on the grounds that he had raped her after
a business banquet in the United States. Despite being subject
to a massive backlash on the internet and not winning her case
based on a lack of "sufficient evidence," Liu Jingyao has won the
unwavering support of the Chinese feminist community, and her
courage has inspired many more survivors to come forward. In
another recent landmark case, 28-year-old Zhou Xiaoxun (popularly known as Xianzi), accused Zhu Jun, one of China's most
prominent TV anchors, of sexually harassing her when she was
an intern. While Zhou also lost her case in September 2021, she
decided to appeal. The huge social impact of her lawsuit, and the
tremendous support she won, demonstrates the potential for a
women's movement to fight sexual harassment. These new radical
organizations and activists tend to have explicit agendas, pushing
for institutional accountability and using court cases to fight for
justice and reforms.

Beyond this, there is a broader women's reaction, most tan-
gible as a form of sentiment, to the state's pronatalist campaign
to reinstate women's "traditional" social role as having babies,
providing care in the family, and doing domestic labor. Coined
"Made-in-China Feminism," it lacks organization, does not have
a clear political agenda, and tends to respond to these pressures in
an individualistic fashion.[17] There are two strands within "Made-
in-China Feminism." The first is an entrepreneurial one in which
women cultivate a hyperfeminine image in an attempt to marry up
the class ladder. The second is more oppositional. Women in this
strand reject marriage and the reproductive role being imposed on

women, and instead pursue individual achievement and career advancement. The second strand has become more typical, making it very unlikely that the state will be able to push all women back to the family to have more kids anytime soon.

STRATEGIC SITES OF STRUGGLE AND SOLIDARITY

Thus, Chinese capitalism's social reproductive crisis is generating a variety of feminist struggles and movements. And more could emerge in the coming years, including among working-class women. Here are a few likely areas where we can expect resistance. First, in the domestic labor market. Urban families rely on hired domestic labor for their social reproduction, giving these predominantly female workers a good deal of structural bargaining power. This power will only be enhanced by labor market dynamics, as the megacities are no longer seeing huge inflows of young people from the countryside and rural women are also more reluctant to leave their own children behind.[18] Despite the informal character of these jobs, these workers have the capacity to organize and resist their oppression and exploitation.

Second, women play a pivotal role in the rest of the economy and therefore have tremendous potential economic power to resist their increasing oppression. Notwithstanding the state's "family values" discourse, women's average educational level has reached a historic high and their labor force participation, despite recent declines, remains one of the highest in the world. This is likely to remain the case as the economy shifts from traditionally male-dominated industries, like manufacturing, construction, and agriculture, toward services, which have much higher rates of female employment. The combination of the state pressure for women to take up more reproductive labor and the economy's dependence on their labor will stoke resistance among women workers for change that addresses their demands for improved conditions at work as well as demands for gender equality.

The state seems to be aware of this danger and has taken steps to tamp down resistance. For example, in July 2021, the state issued a new policy that promotes gender-based affirmative action in the field of science and technology. This is a very limited measure that falls far short of what is needed and will likely only impact middle-class women. It is clearly meant to co-opt struggle from below, but it could easily backfire and trigger more struggle. The mere fact that the state had to address women's grievances is likely to encourage demands for more change, especially because policy is so insufficient for those that it applies to and because it leaves most women out.

Finally, and perhaps most importantly, the political-economic roots of the social reproduction crisis are driving a convergence among Chinese feminists, labor activists, and liberal-leaning political dissidents—a phenomenon that was not imaginable a decade ago. There is a growing recognition that such a convergence is not only morally good but also strategically necessary. China's class inequality, gender oppression, and denial of democratic rights are not separate issues; they are profoundly interrelated. Take, for example, the labor and political protests against China's draconian COVID policies. The state imposed "closed-loop management" on workers and brutal lockdowns in cases where outbreaks occurred, both of which were designed to keep the economy functioning amid the pandemic and protect "normal life" for the privileged.

The main victims of these policies were women, who were tasked with even more responsibility for social reproduction amid lockdowns, as well as migrant workers in "closed-loop" factories, ethnic minorities, especially Uyghurs, the elderly, and the sick.[19] They were all driven to resist. Militant workers, students, medical workers, and young women fearlessly organized strikes and demonstrations against the authorities.[20] In these uncoordinated actions of the exploited and oppressed, there is an implicit basis for united struggle to challenge the status quo. That threat, combined with evident failure of Zero-COVID to stop the spread of the pandemic, forced the state into a hasty retreat, reopening China domestically and internationally with the dual aim of quelling the resistance and spurring growth in the economy. The opportunity and challenge for the new feminist movement in China and, indeed throughout the world, is to forge a united front of workers and the oppressed against the crisis-ridden capitalist order.

CHAPTER 5

CHINA'S NATIONAL QUESTIONS

Protests within China's core have been common, and often militant, but remain highly fractured and largely refrain from articulating explicit political aims. Outside "China proper," however, conditions have become much more volatile and struggle more explosive and sustained. From 2008 to 2020, China's periphery was the site of intense social resistance. This twelve-year sequence witnessed massive upheavals in Tibet, Xinjiang, and Taiwan. Hong Kong has seen two spectacular bouts of mass insurgency, first in 2014 and then again in 2019. There were distinct fuses for each of these events, and the issues highlighted by protesters were similarly varied. But in sharp contrast to the character of protest in China's core regions, these were all marked by overt hostility to the Chinese state, as well as a willingness to employ radical tactics, up to and including violent confrontation with the police.

In order to understand these recurrent bouts of unrest at precisely the moment China emerged as a global superpower, it is important to first grasp some features of governance in China. Particularly since Deng Xiaoping came to power, state legitimacy has been constructed on two pillars: regular improvements in living standards and ethnonationalist pride in China's rise. Decades of rapid growth have helped the state deliver economic benefits to a broad base—even as inequality soared from the 1990s on, most people saw at least marginal improvements in livelihoods. As economic growth has slowed in recent years, Xi Jinping has leaned increasingly on ethnonationalism, enshrining the "great revival of the Chinese nation" as the state's overarching aim. These two strategies have been largely successful. Despite disaffection from many intellectuals, lawyers, and activists, indicators are that Xi is popular even among those classes that have not gained significantly from China's capitalist development.

While these pillars of legitimacy have held up public support in China's Han-dominated core, they crumble in its periphery and near abroad, particularly in Tibet, Xinjiang, Hong Kong, and Taiwan. While conditions vary widely in each of these places, they share some common elements. Most importantly, deeper integration with the Chinese state has overwhelmingly benefited elites in all four regions, while leaving most peasants as well as working-class and poor people behind. In Tibet and Xinjiang, Han settlers have captured most of the rewards from increased infrastructure spending and economic activity. As both Hong Kong and Taiwan drew economically closer to China during the late twentieth and early twenty-first centuries, real estate tycoons, financiers, and big manufacturing interests cashed in, while most people faced the loss of manufacturing jobs, stagnating wages, and out-of-control housing prices. Finally, few people in these regions derive a sense of national pride from Han China's increasing wealth and power—indeed, it is seen as a threat to established culture, social patterns, and ways of living. As a result, the PRC's assertion of ethnonationalism in its periphery has triggered struggles for self-determination, which the state has responded to with violent repression, forced assimilation, and militarization.

SITUATING HAN NATIONALISM

Nationalism in China developed in the late nineteenth and early twentieth centuries in response to European, and later Japanese, colonial and imperialist aggression. The idea of "China" as a coherent nation was articulated by intellectuals at the end of the Qing dynasty as a means for advancing independence and modernization. But this would not be straightforward, for as Arif Dirlik has argued, "Contemporary names for 'China,' *Zhongguo*, or *Zhonghua* have a history of over two thousand years, but they were neither used consistently nor had the same referents at all times."[1] Sun Yat-sen, hailed as the father of the nation by the PRC and Republic of China alike, was committed to a modern Chinese state, and further specified a revolutionary platform based on Han identity. The Han ethnicity is hugely diverse, containing a wide array of languages, cuisines, and religious practices spread over a vast territory. In Sun's formulation, the majority Han would be the core of the new Chinese nation-state after deposing the Manchurian Qing Empire. In the 1950s, the PRC designated fifty-six officially recognized ethnicities: today, 92 percent are Han and the remaining population is made up of the fifty-five ethnic minorities, largely concentrated on the peripheries of the country.

While there is no question that the early CCP was committed to class politics, nationalism has always been a key component of its agenda. This was a reasonable response to a situation in which capitalism was largely introduced by imperialist powers. It also meant, however, that Han nationalism was baked into the DNA of the party, and the distinct interests of other ethnicities could be, and were, marginalized. Since the Party's refusal to acknowledge class antagonism in the era of market reforms, the leadership has leaned much more heavily on Han nationalism. It is more than apparent today that the Han are the unmarked norm to which other ethnicities must bend within the formally inclusive "Chinese nation" (*zhonghua minzu*) of official rhetoric. Furthermore, with the interests of the Party and the nation represented as synonymous, dissent from the state is equated with being a race traitor. Hence the common epithet *hanjian*—"traitor to the Han"—hurled at Chinese people who question the total authority of the state.

RESISTANCE TO EXTERNALLY IMPOSED "DEVELOPMENT" IN TIBET

Tibet has been one of the key places of resistance to Han Chinese colonialism. It has a long and complex history of relationships with successive premodern Chinese empires. Han (as well as Mongolian and Manchu) control of the Tibetan plateau has waxed and waned, but with the fall of the Qing Empire in 1911, Tibet was indeed independent. The newly established Republic of China—and its still unborn successor, the People's Republic of China—maintained claims to the region, based on its historical incorporation within the Qing Empire. Following military invasion, the PRC's rule over Tibet was formalized in a 1951 agreement. In the years that followed, Tibetan resistance to Chinese colonialism was a persistent issue. While this opposition was by all means just, the CIA tried to co-opt the Tibetan struggle for self-determination to undermine CCP rule. The 1959 uprising in Lhasa was the dramatic culmination of years of growing resistance elsewhere on the plateau, and it provoked a violent crackdown by Chinese authorities, with the Dalai Lama fleeing to India where he established a government in exile.

Official PRC discourse has long had strong colonial characteristics. The CCP claimed it liberated Tibet from barbaric feudalism and carried out its modernization. But there is no question that control of Tibet is not motivated by altruism: the region is of critical strategic importance, given China's at times conflictual relationship with India, and it is also rich in minerals and the headwaters of numerous major rivers. While it is important to avoid a fetishized image of Tibet's past as some sort of Buddhist mountain utopia—an alluring vision to many Westerners—Tibetans themselves have continually chafed under Chinese rule. More recently, the state has extolled its own beneficence in building infrastructure and developing the capitalist economy.[2] The paternalistic expectation is that Tibetans will express gratitude for such material improvements, while forsaking presumably backward superstitions (not to mention their attachments to the exiled Dalai Lama).

Whether or not broad-based economic improvement would be sufficient to blunt Tibetans' concerns about loss of religion and cultural identity is an open question. However, even the state's claims that development has improved their material well-being are overblown. Although the region's GDP growth has been impressive, most good jobs and entrepreneurial opportunities have gone to Han settlers. Resources for quality education and health care continue to be disproportionately funneled to the largest, wealthiest cities, which are without exception Han-dominated spaces. Anti-Tibetan discrimination in the labor market is well documented, a phenomenon that is nationwide in scope.[3] While the government lauds its own success in anti-poverty initiatives, practically speaking this has often meant forced relocation from rural areas into small towns and cities. Even if some housing arrangements are made for the displaced, Tibetans often find it extremely difficult to incorporate into urban (and capitalist) work regimes. A large percentage of Tibetans are illiterate, and once relocated to cities their social resources are diminished or eliminated.[4]

Such forced relocation also plays a key colonial role. It disrupts and often shatters Tibetan social structure, thereby undermining the basis of resistance. Han settlers in Tibetan regions have been the overwhelming beneficiaries of expanded government spending on infrastructure—and these projects themselves often entail the dislocation and dispossession of Tibetan populations. And as is always the case in a colonial setting, infrastructural expansion is not simply for advancing economic growth, but also for consolidating political control.

Perhaps more significant has been the government's efforts to impose cultural control. The CCP's deep animosity for the Dalai Lama is well-known, despite the Tibetan leader having long ago asserted that he no longer advocates Tibetan independence. Worshiping the Dalai Lama or displaying his image is banned, and the government has imposed strict regulation over monasteries and all forms of religious practice. The CCP has preemptively asserted that the Dalai Lama's reincarnation must comply with Chinese law, meaning that the state reserves the right to determine his successor.

This loss of cultural autonomy has been paired, not coincidentally, with an effort to sanitize and repackage Tibetan culture as a commodity for (largely Han) tourist consumption.[5] As might be imagined, cartoonish representations of traditional culture have done little to inspire a sense of self-worth.

The failure of these efforts to extinguish simmering resentment at Han colonial rule burst into the open in 2008. In the run-up to that year's Olympic games in Beijing, Tibetan monks began gathering in Lhasa to commemorate the anniversary of the 1959 uprising. Massive and sometimes violent protests erupted in Lhasa and elsewhere on the Tibetan plateau. In response to police repression, big protests greeted the Olympic torch processions in cities around the world.

In the years that followed, the state turned to repression to stop the wave of public protests. Chen Quanguo—now notorious for having developed the system of internment camps in Xinjiang— honed his brutal statecraft in Tibet, where he served as Party secretary from 2012 to 2016. With public protests extremely risky, Tibetans tried different modes of resistance. Some turned to self-immolation as the only form of escalation possible while conforming to the Dalai Lama's call for nonviolence. At least 159 Tibetans set themselves on fire between 2009 and 2019.[6] Faced with ongoing protests, the state intensified methods of control. Recently, it subjected hundreds of thousands of Tibetans to "labor transfer" programs that are frequently coercive in nature. Overt resistance has been quelled for the moment, but the underlying political problems have not been resolved.

The Tibet issue has long been challenging for the left outside of China. The Dalai Lama is a complex figure, having himself embraced US and other Western powers, as his collaboration with the CIA testifies. Particularly in the 1990s, Tibet received a lot of attention from liberals and glitzy celebrities, and the region remains of geopolitical interest to US imperialism. But despite having unsavory supporters in the West, the left must understand the situation from the Tibetan standpoint and *as experienced by them*: there is no question that Tibet is subject to colonial rule by the PRC, which has undermined its cultural and economic autonomy. Forced relocations are a form of primitive accumulation meant to free up land and incorporate Tibetans as exploitable laborers. Faced with such national oppression, Tibetans have the right to self-determination and the right to shape their own future as they see fit.

ANTI-TERRORISM AND THE SETTLER COLONIAL PROJECT IN XINJIANG

Xinjiang's colonial character is reflected in its very name—in Mandarin its literal meaning is "new frontier." This hints at its relatively recent incorporation into China; it came under control of the Manchu-run Qing Empire only in the eighteenth century. An independent nation of East Turkestan was established during the Republican era, but after 1949 the new PRC asserted irredentist claims to the region based on the borders of the old empire. Formally designated as the Xinjiang Uyghur Autonomous Region, China's stated policy endorsed a multiethnic society and granted significant cultural autonomy to minorities. Nonetheless, the central government was anxious about political control of the Uyghur-majority region from the outset, and the Xinjiang Production and Construction Corps (better known as the *Bingtuan*) was established as a semimilitary entity to facilitate Han settlement and economic activity in Xinjiang.

Uyghurs, who are indigenous to the region, speak a Turkic language and have practiced Islam for centuries. Although Uyghurs constituted a very large majority of the population of Xinjiang at the founding of the PRC, the region has long been home to diverse groups, including Kazakhs, Hui, Mongols, and of course Han. Since the 1950s, the state has orchestrated numerous efforts to encourage permanent Han settlement in the region, which it sees as a critical step to guaranteeing political stability. This settler colonial effort has resulted in a dramatic increase in the Han population in Xinjiang. As a result, Uyghurs are a plurality of the population and have fallen below 50 percent as the Han are catching up.

Over the past two decades, the Chinese state has tried to incorporate the interior and western part of the country by allowing these regions to cash in on its economic ascendance. Xinjiang has been no exception. The central government has financed major infrastructure projects and incentivized private investment in the region. More recently, the Belt and Road Initiative, which aims to expand infrastructure and economic exchange between China and central Asia (among other regions), has given Xinjiang new strategic significance. As with countless other colonial projects, the state assumes that the benefits of capitalist development will blunt demands for self-determination.

Uyghurs, however, have benefited little from Xinjiang's impressive economic growth, whose spoils have largely gone to Han settlers. This racial inequality is the product of discrimination in schooling and the labor market. Advancing in China's system of higher education requires mastery of Mandarin, which puts native Uyghur-speakers (as well as speakers of Tibetan, Kazakh, and other minority languages) at a distinct disadvantage. Equally important is that the education system funnels resources to elite spaces—public primary and middle schools in Beijing are worlds away from that of rural Xinjiang. Those Uyghurs and other minorities that *are* able to master Mandarin, excel in secondary education, and gain access to tertiary education, will still face pervasive racial discrimination in the labor market. As in countless other colonial situations, even absent malicious intent from the dominant ethnic group, good paying white-collar jobs are largely inaccessible to the subordinate races. Uyghurs remain confined to low-end service and manufacturing work, as well as agriculture.

This subordinated position was dramatically exposed in a series of events that would result in tragic race riots in 2009. That year, a group of Uyghur workers had been brought to Guangdong province as a cheap source of factory labor. A rumor began to circulate among Han workers that a Uyghur had raped a Han woman, leading to a violent physical altercation between the two groups of workers. At least two Uyghurs were killed in the fracas. This, in turn, led to Uyghur protests in the provincial capital of Ürümqi, as people demanded justice for the murdered workers. When police tried to suppress the protests, things spiraled out of control, leading to days of race riots, during which dozens of both Uyghur and Han residents were killed.

Following this social eruption, a low-level and occasionally violent insurgency simmered for years. Uyghurs engaged in numerous knife attacks on police stations in Xinjiang. In 2013, two people were killed when Uyghurs drove a car loaded with explosives into a crowd in Tiananmen Square. Then, in an event that would trigger escalating state repression, thirty-one people were killed in a terror attack at a train station in Kunming in 2014. Taking a cue from George W. Bush, the state launched what it called the "People's War on Terror" to root out "Islamic extremism."

Over the next several years, the security apparatus unleashed an intense campaign to subjugate and collectively punish the PRC's Muslim citizens.[7] By 2017, the state had constructed massive camps, euphemistically referred to as "re-education centers," where it jailed hundreds of thousands of Muslims.[8] While the pretense was that these were merely job training sites, extensive leaks as well as publicly available government documents have revealed that the camps were intended to promote "de-radicalization" and a sense of "ethnic unity," as well as submission to CCP rule. Myriad minor infractions could land someone in the camps, including excessive religiosity (as determined by the state), traveling internationally, maintaining contact with people outside of the country, or efforts to document, preserve, and disseminate Uyghur culture. Nearly every prominent Uyghur intellectual or artist that did not hew closely to the Party line ended up in the camps or faced charges of separatism. The latter charge was given even to those Uyghurs actively supporting Uyghur-Han dialogue and peaceful coexistence, such as prominent academic Ilham Tohti or former Xinjiang University president Tashpolat Tiyip.[9]

The state's attack on Uyghur culture has not been limited to the camps and the prisons. It has created a dystopian system of surveillance throughout Xinjiang that tightly controls all digital activities, and even tracks individuals' movements through cities and towns with an encompassing system of security cameras linked to facial recognition software.[10] In echoes of apartheid-era South Africa or the contemporary West Bank, Uyghurs cannot travel through their homeland without being constantly subjected to police searches and harassment, while Han residents are allowed to go about their business relatively unperturbed. The state has taken seemingly vindictive measures to erase, sanitize, or Sinicize sites of cultural significance. This has included the renovation or destruction of mosques and graveyards in multiple locations. Finally, Uyghur language education has come under immense pressure, as instruction in the language itself has come to be viewed as a threat to interethnic unity.

There are yet more sinister initiatives that suggest a coordinated effort to reduce the Uyghur population. According to government statistics, birth rates fell precipitously in the region from 2018, and even more so in predominantly Uyghur parts of the province.[11] The number of IUDs distributed similarly shot up in the same period of time, far outpacing rates in Han-majority parts of the country. These developments are not spontaneous. The government issued official proclamations dating back to 2014 about the need to control birth rates among Uyghurs. It has also offered monetary incentives for Han and Uyghurs to marry, with the assumption that the children will be assimilated as Han. An unknown but large number of Uyghur children have been taken from their parents. In some cases, the government has interned parents and placed their children in Mandarin-language only boarding schools. Because of government restrictions on independent investigations, the full extent of the repression, internment, forced relocation, and compelled assimilation cannot be determined. But, based on individual testimonies, satellite imagery, leaked documents, as well as the government's own data and proclamations, it is clear that the Uyghurs face an existential crisis.[12]

China has imposed this carceral nightmare on Xinjiang by piggybacking on Washington's Global War on Terror and in collaboration with global capital. Beijing took advantage of the US State Department decision in 2002 to list the East Turkestan Islamic

Movement—a group Beijing dubiously claimed was responsible for dozens of attacks—as a terrorist organization. The Bush administration did this with the hopes of blunting Beijing's opposition to the war in Iraq. China used that classification and the Islamophobic anti-terrorism framework to dehumanize Uyghurs. As late as 2018, Donald Trump reportedly told Xi Jinping he supported the government's measures in Xinjiang. And numerous US and European corporations have benefited from the forced-labor regimes associated with the camps, most notably in the garment and apparel sector. US tech companies such as Oracle have sold technology that has aided the Chinese state in constructing their fearsome police surveillance capacity. In short, while the tragedy in Xinjiang is of course of the Chinese state's making, Washington's Global War on Terror has enabled it and transnational capital has profited from it. Only a robust rejection of Islamophobia, uncompromising opposition to Han settler colonialism, and commitment to political self-determination of indigenous people can resolve this social catastrophe.

REVOLT AND REPRESSION IN HONG KONG

From 1842 to 1997, Hong Kong was a British colony. Under its rule, British imperialism imposed one of the world's most radical free-market experiments and kept democratic rights and institutions highly constrained. As a result, Hong Kong has consistently ranked at or near the top of the Heritage Foundation's Index of Economic Freedom. While the colonial regime facilitated the free movement of commodities and financial capital, it allowed workers few labor rights, instituted no minimum wage, and didn't even provide a public pension system. Collective bargaining rights were passed by the Legislative Council mere days before the 1997 handover, only to be repealed almost immediately after returning to PRC rule.

The colonial governor of Hong Kong was appointed by the British monarch. By the end of colonial rule, a portion of seats in the

Legislative Council were directly elected, with other seats designated as indirectly elected "functional constituencies" that represented government-designated special interests—the majority of which were commercial in nature. Despite the undemocratic and overwhelmingly capitalist nature of the colonial regime, an independent judiciary and robust civil society protections were institutionalized. Freedom of association, freedom of the media, and freedom of speech were largely protected.

As the twilight of Britain's rule in Hong Kong came into view, Deng Xiaoping and Margaret Thatcher signed the "Sino-British Joint Declaration" in 1984. It laid out the rules governing the handover of the city that had since the nineteenth century been a key entrepôt for Euro-American capitalism in East Asia. The core principle was that Hong Kong would be governed as a Special Administrative Region (SAR) of the PRC under the principle of "one country, two systems." While national defense and diplomacy would become Beijing's domain, Hong Kong would maintain a "high degree of autonomy" in managing its own affairs for a period of fifty years following the handover in 1997. The Hong Kong SAR government was to have its own mini-constitution—the Basic Law—and could maintain its political and legal system, its free-market economics, as well as its liberal civil society, media, and education system.

Much of Hong Kong's bourgeoisie had undoubtedly been worried about the return to a self-proclaimed socialist state. This anxiety was further sharpened in broad swaths of Hong Kong society after the Tiananmen massacre in 1989. Even prior to the handover on July 1, 1997, Beijing's strategy for incorporating Hong Kong began to come into view. They focused on courting the powerful oligarchs that ran the city and convincing them, as well as smaller industrial capitalists, that they would become enriched by deeper integration with the Mainland. Giving the lie to China's claim to socialism, the interests of Hong Kong's working classes and ethnic minorities were simply not a consideration. Beijing's strategy worked exceedingly well in co-opting elites and ensuring a relatively smooth interimperial transfer of sovereignty—one accomplished with no participation or input from the overwhelming majority of Hong Kong's citizenry.[13]

Since its return to PRC rule, Hong Kong has experienced wave after wave of mass social resistance. The opening salvo was the successful 2003 movement against Article 23, an anti-subversion legislation that would have dramatically undermined civil liberties. Regular protests of several hundred thousand people have been held on July 1, the date commemorating the handover, for many years after. Smaller-scale movements developed over the 2000s and early 2010s, including movements against a planned Disneyland, anti-development movements, the youth-led actions against "patriotic education," and a huge strike by dockworkers in 2013. The 2014 umbrella movement and 2019 anti-extradition bill movement captured global headlines as the city experienced two mass social revolts within the span of five years.

The basic political contradiction that has produced such intense movement activity is this: Hong Kong citizens had civil rights, but only highly constrained political rights. Until recently, they were free to speak their mind and freely associate into organizations, unions, and political parties, but the Legislative Council and chief executive remained firmly under the control of Beijing-allied capitalists and their subservient politicians. Hong Kong people have continually voiced demands through political parties and mass movements against a state that is insulated from democratic accountability and therefore unresponsive to popular demands.

As a result, state policies have only benefited the already wealthy, while Hong Kong's majority have experienced economic stagnation or downward mobility. In addition to finance, which has long been the cornerstone of the city's economy, the HKSAR (Hong Kong Special Administrative Region) has focused heavily on attracting real estate investment and tourism from Mainland China. From the perspective of elites, this has been very successful, as Hong Kong has become the most expensive real estate market in the world. The facilitation of this investment from China has greatly enriched the few oligarchs who had secured access to valuable land rights under colonial land arrangements.

In order to cater to wealthy tourists, much of the city's commercial property has been re-oriented toward luxury goods and other high-end commodities. These economic priorities of finance, commercial real estate, and tourism have reduced employment opportunities for the large majority of Hong Kong people to low-end service-sector jobs. These are almost entirely union-free and pay only the pitifully low minimum wage. Living at the edge of poverty, it is completely impossible for working-class and even most middle-class people in the city to consider buying an apartment. With public housing woefully inadequate, people are forced to squeeze into tiny apartments with exorbitant rents.

While these conditions are the source of economic grievances, the key issues that caused the explosion of protests in 2014 and 2019 were political and cultural issues. Since the handover, the chief executive (CE) has been elected by an unrepresentative election committee composed overwhelmingly of economic elites and Beijing loyalists. Carrie Lam, the CE from 2017 to 2022, was originally "elected" with just 777 votes in a city with 7.5 million residents. The 1984 joint declaration had promised that at an indeterminate time in the future, the CE would be elected by universal suffrage. Beijing announced in 2014 that it would follow through on this pledge, but that the candidates could only be nominated by a tightly managed committee. Thus, the central demand of the massive umbrella movement was to implement "real universal suffrage," in other words, an electoral system in which political parties could freely nominate their own candidates.

That movement failed to attain its goal, and the issue of democracy was still unresolved in 2019 when Carrie Lam tried to push through a hugely unpopular extradition bill. It would have allowed Hong Kong to extradite suspected criminals to Mainland China to face trial. Hong Kongers, and particularly political activists, were understandably anxious at the prospect of being sent to the CCP-controlled, and notoriously nontransparent-Mainland judicial system. But amid broader concerns about Hong Kong's citizens' ability to maintain whatever democratic rights they had, the extradition bill ended up sparking one of the most militant, spectacular, and sustained social revolts of the twenty-first century. The primary goals of the movement, in addition to defeating the extradition bill, were opposition to astonishing police violence as well as the unmet demand for genuine universal suffrage.

Hong Kongers have also been keenly aware of intensifying ethnonationalism in the CCP, with its attendant rigid definition of patriotism and fealty to the state. They have seen how cultural expression that falls outside the bounds of Party-defined norms has been crushed—most brutally in Tibet and Xinjiang. They have watched the state eliminate non–Mandarin Chinese languages (even for Han people), something that has generated resistance even across the border in Cantonese-speaking Guangdong province. As poignantly depicted in the wildly successful film *Ten Years*, Hong Kongers are acutely aware that their unique culture is seen as a threat by the Chinese state, and that deeper integration would mean forced assimilation into a version of Chineseness that they do not identify with. Indeed, the past several years have witnessed plunging numbers of people in Hong Kong who see themselves as "Chinese," while an increasing number identify as "Hong Konger."[14] This is particularly notable among young people who may have weaker ties to the Mainland than is the case for their parents and grandparents.

Despite more than half a year of sustained mass unrest, including one event with protesters that included 25 percent of the entire population of Hong Kong, the movement was defeated through overwhelming and brutal police violence. In the wake of this repression, Beijing pushed through a draconian National Security Law. Since then, freedom of speech has been throttled, opposition parties have been disbanded or functionally eliminated from participation, independent unions disbanded, and activists of all sorts arrested and jailed. A parallel legal process has been institutionalized for national security, separate from the traditional legal system and whatever independence and integrity it may have left. The limited forms of democratic participation that existed previously have all but been extinguished. Amid this tidal wave of reaction, tens of thousands of political activists and others unable to imagine a decent future in the city have fled into exile. In 2023 the Hong Kong government offered a bounty of HK $1,000,000 (≈ US $127,650) for the capture of certain exiled activists, including former Hong Kong Confederation of Trade Unions leader Mung Siu-tat.

The 2019 movement created much confusion in the US and Western left more broadly, for understandable reasons. Although many felt immediate sympathy for an avowedly pro-democracy movement, vociferous support for Hong Kong from Sinophobic politicians such as Josh Hawley, Tom Cotton, and Ted Cruz muddied the waters. Despite Trump's equivocation—he once told reporters, "We have to stand with Hong Kong, but I'm also standing with President Xi. He's a friend of mine"—much of the US right embraced the movement, certainly not because of a steadfast commitment to democracy, but rather as a means to mobilize under the tired banner of anti-communism. Further complicating matters was the relatively small, but quite vocal segment of Hong Kongers who waved US and British flags at protests and openly embraced Trump with the hope of mobilizing US support for their cause.

While it would be wrong to ignore this right-wing, pro-US, and Sinophobic current within Hong Kong's social movement arena, it is important to recognize that the majority of movement protesters do *not* hold such political positions. The core demands of the movement, repeated at protest after protest throughout 2019, were for an expansion of democracy and opposition to police brutality. These are demands that the left should support wherever they appear. Nearly all of Hong Kong's leftists—including labor, ethnic minorities, environmentalists, feminists, and queer activists—fully supported the movement, as they understood they had the most to lose from the erosion of democracy. A movement that incorporates such huge swaths of a population is bound to have political heterogeneity. As long as the core demands are progressive, the international left should support it and help the left exercise leadership within the movement. The Hong Kong left, much of it now in exile, faces a long struggle against an increasingly authoritarian, pro-Beijing HKSAR government. They will need our support and solidarity in the years to come.

TAIWAN: THE STRUGGLE FOR SELF-DETERMINATION AMID IMPERIAL CONTESTATION

Taiwan is a rather different case from Hong Kong, Xinjiang, and Tibet for many reasons, most importantly because it is not under the jurisdiction of the People's Republic of China. The Communist Party has never exercised control of the island, and the Republic of China (Taiwan), as it is formally known, maintains its own system of government. But Taiwan fits in this section on the national question because Beijing sees annexation of it as perhaps *the* key step in completing its national rejuvenation. Nonetheless, given its de facto independent status, politics within Taiwan are quite distinct from the other regions discussed here.

The indigenous people of Taiwan speak Austronesian languages and have inhabited the island for thousands of years. The island was first colonized in the early seventeenth century by the Dutch in the southern and western regions while the Spanish had a small outpost in the north. The first major Han migration to the island happened under Dutch rule beginning in the seventeenth century. The Dutch were defeated by a Ming loyalist regime in 1662, and the Manchurian Qing empire defeated the loyalists and incorporated parts of Taiwan by 1683 (though it did not become a province until 1885). Japan wrested Taiwan from the Qing following their victory in the Sino-Japanese war in 1895, which marked the ascendance of the Japanese empire. More than three hundred years of Han in-migration as well as successive waves of imperial contestation remade the social contours of the island, as indigenous people were dispossessed and displaced, rendering them minorities in their homeland.

Established in 1912, the Republic of China (ROC) initially forsook its claim to Japanese-controlled Taiwan. After the entry of the United States into World War II and the growing plausibility of Japan's defeat, the KMT (and then the CCP) raised a revanchist claim to the island based on its earlier incorporation into the Qing empire. Following the US victory in the Pacific, Taiwan indeed was passed to the ROC without consultation of the local population. Taiwanese people encountered the KMT as a brutal occupying force that saw the island as little more than a staging ground for its war with the CCP. Ongoing anger with KMT abuses toward the local population burst into the open during the 228 incident, so named for an anti-government uprising that began on February 28, 1947.

The government responded with brutal repression, killing many thousands and arresting and torturing thousands more. As the KMT faced defeat at the hands of the CCP in the civil war, it fled the Mainland and relocated their government and military forces to Taiwan in 1949, for years maintaining the illusion that they would soon retake all of China. Within Taiwan, the KMT ruled with an iron fist. Dubbed a "white terror," the stridently anti-communist KMT implemented martial law in 1949 that would last for decades.

It was not the brutality of the Chiang Kai-shek regime but rather anti-Soviet geopolitics that led the US to switch recognition from Taipei to Beijing in 1979. Since then, the US has pursued a "One China Policy" which recognizes the Beijing government as the sole representative of China. In contrast, however, to the PRC's "One China Principle," the US does not take a position on whether Taiwan is part of China, and only *acknowledges* but does not *recognize* the PRC's claims over the territory. The policy of strategic ambiguity means that the US has not, until recently at least, stated one way or the other if it would defend Taiwan in the event of war. This was meant to deter PRC aggression as well as avoid emboldening Taiwanese independence activists—indeed, the US has actively sought to tamp down moves toward formal independence. Thus, beginning in 1979, the US maintained unofficial relations with Taiwan while engaging in arms sales and promoting economic and cultural exchanges. Undergirded by US-China consensus on market integration, this framework proved malleable enough to allow for peace across the Taiwan strait for many years. But with the unraveling

of neoliberal globalization, this order has come under increasing
pressure from changing political dynamics in China, Taiwan, and
the US alike.

Amid the geopolitical uncertainty of losing international diplomatic recognition, Taiwan's pro-democracy movement became increasingly mobilized during the 1980s. In response to pressure from
below, as well as a desire to secure support from Western states, in
1987 Chiang Ching-kuo (Chiang Kai-shek's son) ended martial
law and initiated a process of political liberalization. Democratization in Taiwan has without a doubt been a positive development.
It allowed not only for competitive elections, but also for greater
civil rights, including the establishment of independent political
parties, unions, and other progressive social movement organizations. These movements have notched some important, if partial,
victories. Taiwan has initiated a reckoning with its autocratic past,
and while the KMT still commands significant economic and political resources, it has become significantly constrained. In 2016,
President Tsai Ing-wen of the Democratic Progressive Party (DPP)
issued an apology to Taiwan's indigenous people for their historical oppression. Perhaps most famously, Taiwan became the first
nation in Asia to allow for same-sex marriages in 2019. There are
important critiques of the shortcomings of these social and political
changes. Nonetheless, in an era marked by retreat from even basic liberal democratic rights globally, Taiwan has made important
marginal advances.

Taiwan's class politics, on the other hand, have been much
more in line with the global trend. With the important exception
of establishing high-quality national health insurance in 1995,
free-market reforms and their attendant social precarity have advanced significantly in recent decades. Despite some internal political heterogeneity, the main opposition party, the DPP, more or less
bought into the neoliberal consensus of the 1990s. Immediately
following political democratization, Taiwan witnessed a wave of
unemployment as many small and medium-sized manufacturers—
the backbone of Taiwan's economic ascendence—relocated to
China and Southeast Asia.

As has been the case in countless other countries, Taiwan's still-nascent labor movement was not able to contain increasingly mobile capital. The service sector has been marked by high levels of inequality, with a small number of highly paid jobs in a sea of low-wage work. Taiwan has some of the highest housing costs in the world, which, much like Hong Kong, has made attaining middle-class status increasingly out of reach for most youth. At the same time that the citizenry is under intense economic pressures, Taiwan has also constructed a highly exploitative guest worker program to bring in people from Southeast Asia to power industries such as manufacturing, fishing, domestic labor, and eldercare. As in many other places around the world, neoliberal capitalism has led to increased inequality, and dim prospects for young people.

Of course, China did not force Taiwan to pursue marketization—Taiwan's own capitalists and political parties were active participants. But Beijing saw an opportunity to make use of the newly mobile Taiwanese capital to bring the country more closely within its orbit. Taiwan's companies have poured huge sums of investment into China's rapidly expanding export-processing zones. The most famous example is Foxconn, which found in China a union-free environment with local government actors able to secure huge swaths of land and gargantuan workforces at low prices. This combination in turn served as the sociopolitical basis for Apple's explosive growth in the 2000s and 2010s, as Taiwanese, Chinese, and US corporations worked hand in glove to extract unbelievable wealth from China's working class. While Foxconn CEO Terry Gou, Taiwan's richest man and recent presidential candidate, has been one of the most visible proponents of closer integration with China, many Taiwanese economic elites are similarly attracted by the vast and exploitable workforce, not to mention the huge market. Ironically, it has been the CCP's old nemesis the KMT that has advocated on behalf of Taiwan's monied elite for deeper integration between the two economies.

Enhanced Taiwan-China economic ties reached a limit in 2014, when a KMT-supported trade deal engendered massive social revolt, dubbed the Sunflower Movement.[15] The "Cross-Strait Services

Trade Agreement" would have brought down restrictions on investment in various service-sector industries, with many predicting that Taiwanese banks would be among the greatest beneficiaries, as they would receive new access to the China market. Huge swaths of the service sector–dominated Taiwanese economy would also have been opened to Chinese investment. In the spring of that year, hundreds of thousands of people flooded the streets, expressing their opposition to a neoliberal trade deal that would enhance China's economic leverage. Hundreds of protesters occupied the Legislative Yuan building for weeks, mobilizing massive public support in a successful effort to derail the trade deal. In a regional context where China has become the dominant capitalist power, deepening marketization appeared to Taiwanese people as almost certainly to lead to an infringement on their democratic rights and self-determination.

The political situation in Taiwan remains tense today. The Sunflower Movement produced a new generation of activists, some of whom are explicitly left-wing in orientation. Some have attempted to build independent political parties, while others have tried to bolster the left wing of the DPP. Taiwan's success with COVID allowed its economy to expand rapidly while many other countries suffered deep crises, but underlying issues of inequality and labor precarity remain. At the same time, China has become more assertive in its claims, sending jets into Taiwan's airspace with increasing frequency. Donald Trump, meanwhile, was transparently trying to use Taiwan as a bargaining chip in his trade negotiations with China. Biden has been something of an enigma on Taiwan, as he has seemingly contradicted the policy of strategic ambiguity by stating repeatedly that the US will defend the country in the event of an attack from Beijing. Staffers have walked back Biden's comments for fear of sparking greater conflict, but it nonetheless appears to be a major shift in US strategy.

The combination of saber-rattling with vacillating US policy adds instability to an already dangerous situation. Nancy Pelosi's 2022 visit to Taiwan, while welcomed by many Taiwanese as a sign of support, brought the conflict between the US and China to new heights. China's militaristic response included shooting missiles over the island (even into Japan's territorial waters) and a massive deployment of warships, which many interpreted as a test run for a naval blockade. This geopolitical jockeying is intensified by Taiwan's indispensable role as a semiconductor producer. TSMC alone accounts for over half of the global semiconductor foundry market, while producing nearly all of the most advanced chips. Contestation over the island is not only motivated by China's nationalism or America's avowed commitment to liberal democracy—Taiwan is an absolutely critical node in the organization of global capitalism.

The international left should categorically oppose militarization and war as the means for resolving this conflict. China must drop its oft-repeated, and legally enshrined, right to use military force against Taiwan. And the US must cease opportunistically using Taiwan as a stick to poke China, without regard for the wishes or well-being of Taiwanese people. As Russia's invasion of Ukraine has shown, military defense can be an important piece of ensuring political autonomy—but a *single-minded* focus on military preparation can also become a self-fulfilling prophecy of spiraling escalation. Given that it is Taiwan's working classes and oppressed who would suffer the most in the event of war, we must follow their lead in charting a path of peace. It is extremely difficult and risky for internationalists from China to speak openly about Taiwan. But those of us outside of China should deepen institutional relationships with Taiwanese society and social movements to push back against the PRC's strategy of international isolation.

And international leftists should support all movements in Taiwan that align with our principles, many of which have nothing to do with China. Indigenous people fighting for territorial and cultural rights, queer activists insisting that the current marriage law is a beginning and not a conclusion, and migrant workers demanding decent labor conditions and political voice are oppressed, first and foremost, by the Taiwanese state. Such connections can and should move in both directions: Taiwanese companies have major overseas investments, including the multibillion-dollar semiconductor fab in Arizona where CEO Morris Chang has sought to avoid hiring union labor.[16] Efforts by those of us in the US or elsewhere to engage with Taiwanese society should be oriented toward advancing these struggles of shared interest, regardless of the geopolitical backdrop.

At the same time, however, the Chinese government has continually asserted its right to use military force to incorporate the island, and the anti-war movement must recognize that the US is not the only nation capable of aggression. It goes without saying that a PRC-controlled Taiwan would lose its civil rights, competitive elections, and independent worker organizations, just as has come to pass in Hong Kong. At least one Chinese official has stated explicitly that Taiwanese people living under occupation would need to be "reeducated,"[17] which many interpreted as meant to evoke the forced assimilation the Uyghurs have endured. It bears repeating that ethnonationalist authoritarian capitalism is not an upgrade from liberal democratic capitalism, even as we try to build movements to transcend the latter. Furthermore, an invasion of Taiwan would also be a catastrophe for the poor and working-class people of China. They would be served up as cannon fodder in a technically challenging sea invasion and military occupation and would bear the brunt of the ensuing diplomatic isolation and economic crisis that would likely follow.

CHINA'S NEW NATIONAL QUESTIONS

Thus, the CCP's open embrace of Han chauvinism and ethnonationalism has detonated struggles for national self-determination in its territory and periphery. This marks a departure from both the Maoist period and its official proclamations on ethnic autonomy, as well as the post-Mao era where the state hoped minorities would be harmoniously incorporated via the benefits of capitalist growth. However, the free market has deepened social hierarchies in Tibet and Xinjiang as Han people have captured the overwhelming benefits of increased growth. Hong Kong and Taiwan, places where capitalist development took off in the mid-twentieth century, have seen stagnating opportunities for most people, and precipitously declining identification with Chineseness. In the three PRC-controlled regions, then, the state has resorted to extreme forms of carceral and police violence to tame movements that reject the ideological hegemony of China's racial capitalism. Taiwan is something of a different story, but the PRC continually asserts its prerogative to resort to military invasion to annex the island.

The international left must not stand on the sidelines of these conflicts. The open embrace of any movement against the CCP by Sinophobic and anti-communist politicians in the West certainly complicates matters. But the right can only relate to these movements in an opportunistic and self-serving manner, and it is clear they maintain no general commitment to the rights of the oppressed. The international left, on the other hand, maintains principles of radical democracy, autonomy, and self-determination for oppressed nations as well as racial and ethnic minorities, and economic equality—all of which have been badly undermined by the Chinese state's approach to the national question. Social movements in these regions are currently at a lull, in large part due to heavy repression and surveillance (here again, Taiwan is distinct). But the underlying problems of social hierarchy, political subjugation, and economic inequality remain. Stuck between an overbearing and uncompromising ethnonationalism emanating from Beijing and opportunistic right-wing authoritarians as well as establishment centrists in the West, movements in China's peripheries for self-determination and democracy will require all the support they can get from the left, unions, and progressive movements.

PART III

IMPERIAL RIVALRY AND CRISES OF GLOBAL CAPITALISM

CHAPTER 6

THE US V. CHINA

The Twenty-First Century's
Central Interimperial Rivalry

A s the conflict over Taiwan makes clear, China's rise as a new capitalist power has brought it into increasing confrontation with the US. Their rivalry involves everything from trade to investment, high-tech production, international affairs, and military hegemony in Asia. Beijing is upsetting the unipolar world order that the US has superintended since the end of the Cold War. China is not alone; Russia, along with a host of regional powers like Iran, Israel, Saudi Arabia, and Brazil to name a fsew, are variously challenging or operating with increasing independence from Washington. This has produced a new asymmetric multipolar world order with a central rivalry between the US and China.

Russia's imperialist war on Ukraine intensified this conflict. Moscow invaded its oldest colony, Ukraine, to lock the country into its sphere of influence, in part as a reaction to the eastern expansion of NATO and the EU. Ukraine responded to Russia's aggression with a mass popular war of national liberation. The US and its allies have supplied Ukraine with weapons and imposed unprecedented sanctions on the Russian state and economy. The Biden administration has used the war to rally its allies not only against Russia, but also against China, which pledged a "friendship without limits" with Moscow during the Beijing Olympics right before the invasion. Washington's reinvigorated global alliance was on full display at the 2022 NATO meetings in Madrid, which included participation from Japan, South Korea, Australia, and New Zealand. The US managed to get NATO—the *North Atlantic* Treaty Organization—to name China as one of its new strategic priorities. It now views Beijing as a "challenge" to "our interests, security, and values" that seeks "to undermine the rules-based international order."[1]

The rivalry between Washington and Beijing had been developing for some time but only became explicit during the Trump administration. Its National Security Strategy documents announced a shift from a focus on the so-called "War on Terror" to "Great Power Competition," naming China and Russia as "revisionist powers" that pose a threat to Washington's hegemony.[2] This shift was not just the product of some erratic decision by a right-wing president, but the result of a growing consensus in the political establishment and at least a section of big business on the need for the US to defend its hegemony against its rising competitor. This consensus explains the fundamental continuity between the Trump and Biden administrations' policy toward China. Indeed, Biden's whole political and economic project is to bolster US economic, military, and geopolitical power to contain China. For its part, Beijing sees the US as its primary antagonist, and has been increasingly willing to confront Washington to ensure its emergence as a global power. This rivalry is opening a new epoch of interimperial conflict that will reshape geopolitics and the world economy.

CAPITALISM AND IMPERIALISM

The roots of the conflict are deeper than this or that leadership of either country. Instead, it is the product of the imperialist logic of global capitalism. Its competitive pressures drive corporations beyond national borders in search of resources, markets, and labor throughout the world. Each capitalist state develops its geopolitical and military power to buttress its corporations' claims in the world economy. Thus, economic competition among capitals tends to produce imperial competition among states for the division and redivision of the world market. These rivalries trigger geopolitical conflict and even war among dominant states, new powers, and oppressed nations. The victors of these conflicts attempt to enforce a new hierarchy among the capitalist states. Some sit atop, others below them, and those at the bottom suffer national oppression, either directly, through colonial rule, or indirectly, through political and economic subjection to the dictates of the most powerful states. Such hierarchies are never permanent. Capitalism's law of uneven and combined development constantly upsets the interstate order. Old powers atrophy, new capitalist powers rise, and they come into conflict as each tries to order the world economy to the advantage of its capitalist class.[3]

As a result, imperialism has produced a sequence of world orders, each with their particular characteristics. First was the classical period of imperialism in the nineteenth and early twentieth centuries, when the great powers, in a multipolar order, conducted an epic scramble for colonial empires, divided up the world, and then fought over its redivision, detonating two world wars, as well as wars of national liberation. The triumph of the US and the USSR in that fratricidal catastrophe produced the bipolar order of the Cold War. These rivals divided up the world into spheres of influence, which were economically segregated from one another, and guarded their territory with nuclear weapons. The risk of mutually assured destruction pushed the conflict into proxy wars and conflicts in the periphery of the system, largely over the process of decolonization and national liberation and which side would claim the allegiance of newly independent states.

With the collapse of the USSR, imperialism and interimperial rivalry did not come to an end. The US emerged as the world's sole superpower astride a unipolar world order. Its dollar became the global currency, its economy was far larger than any others, and its military was more powerful than all other states combined. Washington developed a new bipartisan grand strategy of superintending global capitalism. It believed it could lock in its hegemony by incorporating all the world's states into a neoliberal world order of free-trade globalization. It used the IMF and the World Bank to pry open the world's economies, established the World Trade Organization to cohere an international system of free trade, and deployed the US military, often through the auspices of the UN and NATO, to police so-called rogue states like Iraq, "stabilize" societies like Haiti wrecked by its neoliberal policies, and prevent resistance to its hegemony wherever it appeared. Throughout its reign over the unipolar world order, its top priority was to prevent the rise of any peer competitor.[4]

THE ASYMMETRIC MULTIPOLAR WORLD ORDER

Four developments in the world system undid Washington's unipolar world order. First, the neoliberal boom from the early 1980s to 2008 restructured global capitalism.[5] It produced new centers of capital accumulation, most importantly China, whose economic development enabled it to become a potential rival to the US. Second, Washington's so-called War on Terror bogged the US down in two decades of counterinsurgency in Iraq and Afghanistan. These invasions were intended to assert its control over the Middle East and its strategic energy reserves, and in doing so position it to bully rivals like China, which depend on the region for oil and natural gas. Instead, US defeats in Iraq and Afghanistan dramatically weakened its control over the region and enabled Russia and China to establish independent relations with key oil-producing states in and outside Washington's orbit. Moreover, China took advantage of the US preoccupation with its two interminable occupations to assert its political, economic, and military power in many corners of the world. All of this led General William Odom to call the occupation of Iraq "the greatest strategic disaster in United States history."[6]

Third, the Great Recession of 2008 brought an end to the neoliberal boom, hammering the US and European economies. Their states managed to drag them back from the brink of collapse with

a combination of austerity and stimulus measures, but these policies did not trigger a new boom. Indeed, the system is locked in a
long depression rooted in declining profitability and characterized
by sluggish expansions alternating with deep recessions.[7] China,
by contrast, managed to sustain its massive expansion with an
enormous stimulus package of its own. Its boom propped up the
economies of numerous countries from Australia to Brazil that export raw materials to meet the demand of China's manufacturing
industries, construction of whole new cities, and the building of
advanced modern infrastructure to support this development. As a
result, China was responsible for 40 percent of global growth since
the Great Recession.[8] Of course, China isn't immune from the crisis tendencies of the capitalist system; its state stimulus intensified
its problem of overproduction, overcapacity, government debt, and
speculative investment, most dramatically evidenced by the collapse of the country's largest real estate corporation, Evergrande,[9]
the teetering of another, Country Garden, on the edge of bank-
ruptcy,[10] and the dramatic slowing of its economy in 2023.

Fourth, the pandemic and the global recession it triggered intensified the interimperial rivalry. States all around the world responded with stimulus plans and cheap money policies to restore
growth, but they did not generate a new boom but only a sug-
ar-rush recovery, which was followed by stagnation and rampant
inflation. Faced with slow growth amid the long depression, both
the US and Chinese states have turned to increasingly nationalist
strategies to protect their economies and maintain hegemony over
their discontented populations.

These developments restructured the balance of power among
states in the world system and exacerbated conflicts among them.
The US has suffered relative decline against China and other rivals. As a result, Washington's unipolar moment has been replaced
with a new asymmetric multipolar world order. The US remains
the dominant power with the largest economy, military, and geopolitical influence, but it now faces imperial competitors in the
form of China and Russia as well as increasingly assertive regional
powers, all of which are jockeying for advantage in an increasingly

conflict-ridden state system. The principal rivalry, and the one that will shape all geopolitics and the world economy, is the one between the US and China.

Many call it the New Cold War. While the last one was without a doubt an interimperial rivalry, the analogy is more misleading than illuminating. The USSR and the US and their spheres of influence were economically divided with very little overlap. Today, the US and China are deeply integrated in both economic and geopolitical institutions. US multinationals use China as an export-processing platform, and they covet its enormous market. For their part, Chinese corporations are dependent on exports to US and European markets as well as high-tech imports from the more advanced economies. Moreover, unlike the USSR, China's state-owned and private corporations are challenging US, European, and Japanese capital in key sectors of the world economy. This interdependence and competition produces a much more complex and variegated interimperial rivalry more akin to the dynamics before World War I, the last great period of globalization. But unlike that time, multinational corporations, including Chinese ones, are now much more globally integrated in production, distribution, and sales arrangements. And both states are also tied up in international economic pacts like the WTO and political institutions like the UN. Thus, the asymmetric multipolar world order and its rivalries have distinct characteristics that must be analyzed and understood on their own terms.

FROM "CONGAGEMENT" TO GREAT POWER RIVALRY

This new world order has forced the US to shift its imperial strategy in general and specifically in relation to China. Up until the Trump administration, US policy toward China had been a combination of containment and engagement, or what some policy analysts call "congagement."[11] The US tried to engage and incorporate China into its neoliberal world order and, by doing so, compel it to privatize the rest of its state-owned industries and adopt free-market capitalism. While the stated aim of the US was to encourage China to adopt liberalizing political reforms as well, its quick normalization of relations after the Tiananmen Massacre in 1989 proves that it was far more interested in making profit than democratization. At the same time, Washington remained wary because of Beijing's reluctance to fully follow its dictates and therefore hedged its bets by retaining elements of a policy of containment toward China. For example, it maintained its vast archipelago of military bases in the Asia Pacific and regularly patrolled its waters, including the Taiwan strait, with aircraft carriers and battleships.

The US shifted back and forth between emphasizing the two poles of the "congagement" policy. For example, Bill Clinton's administration called China a "strategic partner," whereas George W. Bush's administration called it a "strategic competitor." Under Barack Obama, the US decisively tilted toward containment with his administration's so-called Pivot to Asia.[12] He hoped to integrate Asia economically into the neoliberal order through the Trans-Pacific Partnership (TPP) agreement, which excluded China. Defense Secretary Ashton Carter declared, "Passing the TPP was as important to me as a new aircraft carrier."[13] To enforce this economic pact, Obama planned to shift 60 percent of the US Navy to the Asia Pacific to deter Beijing's military expansion. Finally, he intended to shore up and expand Washington's historic alliances forged over decades of hegemony in Asia and establish new ones with countries like Vietnam. Obama's Pivot failed. The US remained bogged down in the Middle East, the TPP never even came up for a ratification vote, and its alliances in the Asia Pacific frayed as states doubted Washington's commitment to the region and opted for balancing between the two rivals. Thus, US imperial strategy at the time was at an impasse.

In sharp contrast to Obama, the Trump administration abandoned the overarching strategy of superintending the neoliberal world order, for a new strategy of economic nationalism and "illiberal hegemony."[14] In place of "congagement," it adopted unilateral policies to prosecute "great power competition" with China. While its National Security Strategy also named Russia as a strategic rival,

Trump avoided challenging Moscow for unclear reasons, perhaps because of his affection for right-wing autocrats or appreciation for Vladimir Putin's attempted interference in the US elections. Trump's China policy had economic, military, and geopolitical features. On the economic front, the US abandoned the TPP and multilateral trade deals in general for bilateral ones. He imposed protectionist measures against China, launching a tariff war on its steel and other exports to the US. He tried to end technology transfer between US and Chinese companies, pressure Beijing to privatize its state-owned industries, open the country's markets even more to US multinationals, and stop its state support for national champions in high tech like Huawei.

Trump used national security interests as a rationale to force US high-tech firms to sever their relationships with Chinese companies, and he pushed for US corporations to divert their supply chains out of China. The multinationals, however, remained deeply integrated with China both for production and sale. Most Apple products continued to be manufactured in China[15] and the country remained one of the largest markets for US corporations like GM, Ford, and Tesla.[16] In geopolitics, Trump tried to strong-arm US allies to ban Huawei from their 5G infrastructure as a national security threat. And he attempted to shore up US alliances state by state to prevent China from using its economic might to draw Eurasia under its influence. He also got Japan and Australia to join the "Blue Dot Network," pitched as an alternative to China's BRI.[17] But it remained very much a promissory note with funding of only $60 billion, a sum that paled in comparison to BRI's $1 trillion budget.

On the military front, the US began to retool for conflict with China. It withdrew from the Intermediate-Range Nuclear Forces (INF) treaty with Russia so that it could build more nuclear weapons to close its so-called "missile gap" with China in land-based cruise and ballistic missiles. It ramped up plans to make high-tech weapons to win a possible war with China. In Asia, it launched a new Indo-Pacific strategy to assert US hegemony in the region against China's increased naval power and militarization of islands in the South China Sea. The Trump administration dramatically raised defense spending to build up its land, air, and sea power in the region. It increased weapon sales to allies, including Taiwan. To justify this militarism, Trump and the GOP whipped up nationalist and xenophobic hostility to China.[18] They racialized the pandemic, portraying not just the Chinese government but the Chinese people as enemies. As a result, they triggered a new phase of anti-Chinese racism and a new wave of hate crimes against Chinese and Asian Americans.[19]

But Trump's erratic "America First" strategy largely backfired. His policies continued Washington's relative decline: his explicit bigotry and threat to US democracy with his minions' semifarcical storming of Congress on January 6 compromised Washington's soft power and pretensions to be a model for other countries; his disastrous mismanagement of the COVID emergency prolonged the recession triggered by the pandemic; his transactional approach to international relationships alienated Washington's historic allies; and his belligerence against China only managed to make Beijing even more assertive of its great power ambitions. Instead of "Making America Great Again," Trump accelerated Washington's relative decline. As two Obama administration officials, Robert Malley and Phillip Gordon, wrote, "The Trump saga has projected an image of the United States as demanding of others and unsure of itself, bullying, yet unreliable. The result has been to embolden China, distress Europe and leave all American allies and foes wondering about the durability of our commitments and the credibility of our threats."[20]

BIDEN'S MUSCULAR MULTILATERALISM AGAINST CHINA

To overcome this legacy, Trump's successor, Joe Biden, promised to refurbish Washington's image, restore its power, and reassert its dominion over global capitalism. He carried over Trump's grand strategy of great power rivalry but abandoned his predecessor's toxic unilateralism for a muscular multilateralism, reuniting allies in a "league of democracies" against "authoritarian states" to defend the so-called rules-based, liberal international order of global capitalism. As one of Biden's foreign policy advisors bluntly put it, the new administration's top priorities were "China, China, China, Russia."[21]

To carry out his planned imperial restoration against these rivals, Biden proposed a new industrial policy designed to refurbish the decayed foundations of US capitalism, protect its supply chains through onshoring and "friendshoring," and bankroll the domestic high-tech and green energy development. As Biden put it in his *Interim National Security Strategy Guidance*, his goal was to ensure US supremacy by "building back better at home and reinvigorating our leadership abroad." In rebuilding Washington's power, he continued, "traditional distinctions between foreign and domestic policy—and among national security, economic security, health security, and environmental security—are less meaningful than ever before."[22] Thus, Biden tied all his policies to the reassertion of US imperialism, most importantly against China.

At home, Biden proposed Build Back Better to repair and improve the country's dilapidated infrastructure, upgrade its social infrastructure to ameliorate class and social inequality, and retool institutions like education to better serve corporate interests. Predictably, he only delivered on aspects that business and the centrist establishment supported, like measures to address the pandemic, stimulate economic growth, control inflation, and rebuild hard infrastructure. Most of the promised funding for social infrastructure was left by the wayside. By contrast, Biden has delivered on his promise to bolster Washington's economic, military, and geopolitical strength against Beijing.

First and foremost, he has implemented a new strategy of "de-risking" the US economic relationship with China, partially disconnecting it from key industries with military applications, especially high tech. He maintained and expanded the protectionist regime against China he inherited from Trump, preserving his predecessor's tariffs on Chinese goods. He added more sanctions on Chinese officials and corporations, using their human rights abuses in Hong Kong[23] and Xinjiang as well as ties with the Russian military as justification.[24] In similar nationalist policies, he implemented a series of new "Buy American" executive orders that require the federal government to purchase from US-based manufacturers and increase the percentage of parts made in the US from 55 percent to 75 percent to qualify as "Made in America."[25] He has also encouraged corporations to relocate strategic industries and supply chains with military applications out of China and onshore them in the US or "friendshore" them in allied countries.

His three major bills passed in his first term implemented his industrial policy aimed to enhance US competitiveness in global capitalism and specifically against China. The first of these was the $1.2 trillion Bipartisan Infrastructure Investment and Jobs Act. It plowed money into refurbishing dilapidated roads, railways, and bridges as well as expanding high-speed internet and building new electric vehicle charging stations across the country. Second, he signed the $740 billion Inflation Reduction Act, which has been called the biggest piece of climate legislation in US history. In reality, while the dollar amount seems high, it is spread out over a decade and is about half what the US spends annually on the Pentagon. Thus, it is far too little to redress the ever-intensifying climate emergency.[26] But it does fund the development of solar and wind energy, and electric vehicle manufacturing in an attempt to end dependence on China, which has cornered the market on these industries.

Third, as part of what Chris Miller calls "the chip war,"[27] Biden enacted the CHIPS and Science Act. It is designed to invest $280 billion in corporations and educational institutions to ensure US high-tech supremacy against China.[28] It earmarked $52 billion for domestic chip research and manufacturing and another $170 billion to establish regional technology hubs, STEM education, and research in artificial intelligence, quantum computing, advanced manufacturing, 6G communications, and energy and materials science.[29] In conjunction with this bill, Biden has encouraged high-tech companies to build new chip fabrication plants in the US.

In one example, he secured an agreement with the Taiwanese corporation TSMC, which produces the bulk of advanced high-tech
semiconductors, to open a giant $40 billion plant in Arizona. In
another, Samsung has promised to invest $17 billion in a semicon-
ductor plant in Texas. That is the tip of the iceberg; US companies
are pouring over $200 billion into building other plants across the
country.[30]

Alongside this project of reestablishing and expanding the US
semiconductor industry, Biden has tried to block companies and
countries from enabling China to develop its capacity to produce
high-end chips. Just like Trump, he justified this on the grounds
of national security because of all the military applications of this
technology in weapon systems and fighter planes. He pressured
Taiwan, the Netherlands, and Japan to block transfers of chip
manufacturing machines to China. He doubled down on Trump's
assault on Huawei, restricting its ability to purchase high-end chips
and blocking the use of its hardware in the US and Europe.[31] And,
he issued an executive order instructing the Treasury Department
to prevent US venture capital and private equity firms from funding Chinese companies to develop advanced semiconductors, mi-
croelectronics, quantum computing, and artificial intelligence.[32]

To buttress this assertion of economic power with military
might, Biden increased defense spending specifically to counter
China in the Asia Pacific. His Pentagon budget for 2023 came in
at a whopping $858 billion.[33] He poured money into developing
new high-tech weaponry, missiles, and new bases in Australia, the
Philippines, and elsewhere in the Pacific, all to assert US hegem-
ony over the region and against China. He increased deployment
of the US military in the Asia Pacific to press home the point that
Washington intends to remain the dominant player in the region.
He expanded the Quad alliance with Australia, India, and Japan,
and forged a new trilateral security pact, AUKUS, with Britain and
Australia against China. He promised to expand Washington's Five
Eyes intelligence network, established after World War II by the
US, Britain, Canada, Australia, and New Zealand, to include Ger-
many, India, Japan, and South Korea. He even has managed to get

the latter two to put aside their historic antagonism, rooted in To-kyo's occupation of Korea during World War II, to establish cordial relations and collaborate with the US against China.[34] Finally, as noted earlier, Biden seemed to reverse the policy of "strategic ambi-guity" when he stated that the US would defend Taiwan in the case of an attack—although the White House later insisted that Taiwan policy had not changed.

By bolstering US economic and military power, Biden aimed to strengthen Washington's geopolitical offensive against Beijing. Unlike Trump, Biden adopted a multilateral approach, rallying al-lies together to contain and confront China. As part of that effort, he pushed for the revitalization of the G7, which groups together the most advanced capitalist countries that are US allies, over and above the G20, which includes China and Russia. To counter Chi-na's BRI, Biden, in conjunction with the rest of the leadership of the G7, launched Build Back Better World (B3W) with the promise of hundreds of billions in funds for infrastructure in the developing world. This expands Trump's Blue Dot Network.[35] Connected to B3W, the EU has announced a new Global Gateway with pledged funds of $340 billion for investment in the Global South.[36] Draw-ing on Washington's old Cold War framework, Biden tried to band together a global alliance, a "league of democracies," to confront the so-called authoritarian powers, most importantly China and Russia. He pressured all these states to bend the knee to US dictates to distance themselves from Beijing and Moscow.

Biden's representatives set the tone early during a confronta-tional meeting with Chinese delegates in Anchorage, Alaska, where they made clear Washington's determination to maintain much of Trump's new great power strategy with its accompanying regime of tariffs and sanctions. Soon afterward, the US staged a diplomatic boycott of the Olympic Games in Beijing. All of this weaponiza-tion of human rights reeked of hypocrisy, as the US has its own and ongoing track record of atrocities, most recently in Iraq and Afghanistan, and continues to support serial human rights viola-tors like Saudi Arabia and Israel.

Biden's initial attempts to wield this multilateral power against China got off to a rocky start. He oversaw a shambolic withdrawal of troops from Afghanistan, making the US look weak and incompetent in the eyes of Russia and China. Biden followed this disaster with another: his incompetent inauguration of the new trilateral security pact, AUKUS. With US approval, Britain announced it, along with the sale of nuclear submarines to Australia, scuttling a deal Canberra had previously struck with France for less advanced conventional subs. Caught by surprise at the loss of a $90 billion deal, an outraged France withdrew its ambassadors from all three allies claiming, in the words of its foreign minister, they had been "stabbed in the back."[37]

Biden's so-called "Summit for Democracy," which intended to band one hundred countries together in a new alliance against China and Russia, accomplished little and was easily accused of hypocrisy. It included many states that Freedom House categorized as "partly free," "not free at all," and "electoral autocracies." Notably India, despite its hard ethnonationalist turn under Narendra Modi and his BJP (Bharatiya Janata Party) and their ongoing repression in Kashmir, was on the invite list.[38] At that point, the Biden administration looked weak, ineffective, and wracked by multiple domestic and international crises. Meanwhile, China and Russia, especially after affirmation of their alliance at the Beijing Olympics, looked more confident and assertive.

Russia's barbaric war on Ukraine, however, was a gift to the Biden administration and its imperialist project. It allowed Washington to posture as a defender of an oppressed nation, enabling him to galvanize allies behind an unprecedented sanctions regime against Russia, consolidate the US hold over Europe through the revitalization and expansion of NATO to include Finland and Sweden, and bring the EU closer to Washington's confrontational approach not only toward Russia, but also China. The US moved quickly to use the war to put nations throughout the world on notice that it was willing to use its tremendous geopolitical, economic, and military power to enforce its rule over global capitalism. It pressured states, including China, to adhere to Washington's sanction regime against Russia. And the Biden administration made absolutely clear that while it was for the moment focused on the war in Ukraine, its main priority remained containing and countering China's rise as a great power. As noted above, it got NATO to include China as one of its strategic priorities, and also announced a new trade pact, the Indo-Pacific Economic Framework for Prosperity (IPEF), that's designed to incorporate the region under US economic hegemony.[39]

CHINA'S COUNTERMEASURES

China has countered Washington's shift from "congagement" to great power rivalry by implementing new policies to ensure its continued rise in the world. Faced with global recession and bans on its high-tech corporations, China adopted a new economic strategy of dual circulation, an industrial policy designed to maintain its export industry while at the same time expanding its independent domestic capacities and market. To raise domestic consumption, Xi promised to implement a policy of "common prosperity" and increase wages and benefits for the working class. Far from conceding to Washington and implementing further market reforms, he increased state control over private capital, requiring party minders on corporate boards, and disciplining high-tech moguls like Alibaba's Jack Ma. He doubled down on support for China's high-tech industry, especially in areas that are underdeveloped, like in manufacturing semiconductors, which is currently dominated by Taiwanese and Korean firms.

To neutralize US threats to cut off its supply of such chips, something that would cripple its giants like Huawei, Xi set up a $143 billion semiconductor fund to bankroll research and development, as well as construction of new manufacturing plants, to free it of dependence on Taiwan's TSMC, right now its main supplier.[40] He countered Washington's sanctions on its tech companies by imposing similar ones on US corporations and its allies. For instance, he banned the use of Micron chips by Chinese companies.[41] And he imposed new requirements for foreign companies to secure licenses to import its near monopoly on gallium and germanium, two metals essential for the production of microchips.[42] Finally, to evade US tariffs, Chinese companies have begun to relocate plants to Vietnam, Mexico, and other countries with free-trade deals with Washington.[43]

In response to Washington's increased military pressure, China has raised defense spending to a record high of $293 billion in 2021, according to SIPRI.[44] It accelerated its naval modernization program to project its power into the Asia Pacific. It plans to increase its fleet, already the largest in the world, from 355 to 420 ships, concentrating their deployment in its immediate region.[45] Beijing also stood up to Washington's increased militarism in the Asia Pacific. It has no intention of backing down to the US and conceding its claims to its projected sphere of influence in the region. It deployed its naval vessels in the South China Sea, escalated flights over Taiwan, and staged more air and naval confrontations with the US and other powers' military planes and ships in the region. At the same time, China initiated plans to expand its bases beyond those in the South China Sea. To add to its base in Djibouti, it planned to build another in Equatorial Guinea, which would be its first one in the Atlantic and a direct challenge to the US. On top of these, it is expected to add others in Sri Lanka and Pakistan.[46]

To match Washington's high-tech weapons, China has increased spending on cyberwarfare, satellite surveillance, and nuclear missiles. While the US retains a massive advantage over China in nuclear weapons with a stockpile of over 5,500 warheads, China is on pace to build up a force of 1,000 by 2030.[47] Moreover, Beijing has made a breakthrough in hypersonic weapons capacity, enabling it to penetrate US defense systems. US generals were so surprised by Beijing's new capacity that they called it a "Sputnik Moment," referring to the Cold War space race when the USSR beat the US in successfully launching the first orbital spacecraft.[48]

China responded to Washington's geopolitical bullying in kind. At the first summit with Biden officials in Alaska, Chinese representatives denounced the US for its hypocritical moral lecture about human rights, pointing to its repression of Black Lives Matter protests. The Chinese government placed travel bᵒans on US, EU, UK, and Canadian officials for criticizing its repression of Uyghurs in Xinjiang and their sanctioning of Chinese officials. It also imposed a variety of sanctions on Australia for calling for an inquiry into the origins of COVID. Similarly, it threatened Australia with actions in response to its AUKUS submarine deal.

Xi's best laid plans, just like Biden's, have gone astray. Zero-COVID, which China had hailed as a brilliant policy to suppress the pandemic, blew up in Xi's face, undermining economic growth and triggering mass protest against brutal lockdowns. To get the economy going again, Xi abandoned Zero-COVID and recklessly reopened the economy in the hopes of reviving growth, sickening as much as 80 percent of the population and killing untold numbers of people. The economy recovered to grow at 3 percent in 2022 only to suffer a growing crisis in its real estate sector in 2023 amid overall stagnation. The *Wall Street Journal* went so far as to declare the end of China's forty-year boom.[49] This slowdown has compromised Xi's plans to raise domestic consumption and implement his dual-circulation strategy. His "Common Prosperity" policy has not borne results for the working class, with migrant workers enduring declining wages and young workers suffering unprecedented double-digit unemployment.

Xi's attempt to project global power fared little better. Its pact forged at the Olympics with Russia almost immediately backfired when Putin ordered his troops into Ukraine. The war posed a quandary for China. On the one hand, it wanted to preserve its alliance with Moscow, but, on the other hand, it remained dependent on Europe and North America for export markets and direct investment. As a result, Beijing adopted a contradictory set of positions. It whipped up a domestic propaganda campaign in support of Russia and took advantage of its alliance with Moscow to secure oil deals at discounted prices. And it attempted to deepen relations with regional powers in the Global South that adopted a neutral stance or tacitly backed Russia in the hopes of creating a political bloc against the US.[50] But, at the same time, China abided by Washington's sanctions regime, did not send military aid to Moscow, tacitly encouraged Putin to bring the war to a close, and offered to mediate peace talks.

Xi also tried to placate Washington's ire and maintain the status quo. He gave a speech in favor of globalization at the World Economic Forum at the start of 2023 and tried to lower tensions in the run-up to a planned meeting with US secretary of state Antony Blinken. That, however, was literally blown sky high by "balloongate," when China's high-altitude balloon drifted over the US, eventually to be shot down by a missile fired from a US fighter jet. That incident led to Blinken's trip being postponed and deepened the schisms between the two powers. After months of disengagement, however, they restored contact with reciprocal visits by state functionaries as well as a diplomatic phone call between Biden and Xi.

Despite such feints by both to patch relations up, neither side has shown any sign of backing down in the conflict. Beijing remains determined to prosecute its regional and global ambitions. It escalated its diplomatic push into the Asia Pacific region in the hopes of using its economic relations to secure alliances, security pacts, and basing rights in various countries. It took advantage of the sanctions on Russian oil to purchase it on the cheap. Moreover, it joined Russia to take advantage of the refusal by several states in the Global South to back Washington in its confrontation with Moscow to lure them into their emerging imperial bloc. As part of that effort, Beijing has positioned itself as a deal broker between historic antagonists, establishing accords, for example, between Saudi Arabia and Israel as well as between Israel and the Palestinian Authority.

It has used three new initiatives as part of its Community of Common Destiny to pose alternative international norms to Washington's "rules-based international order." Its Global Development Initiative promises to aid countries in economic development, poverty alleviation, and improvements in health care. It has paired this with its Global Security Initiative, which attempts to establish a principle of "indivisible security"—the idea that no state should establish its security at the cost of another—to guard against Washington's interference in the internal affairs of countries and their

security sphere. Finally, Beijing has launched the Global Civilization Initiative, which calls on countries to refrain from imposing
their values on others. All three are designed to lure countries away
from Washington and into Beijing's sphere of influence. As part of
that effort, Beijing pushed for the expansion of its BRICS alliance
to include Iran, Saudi Arabia, Egypt, Argentina, the UAE, and
Ethiopia in an open challenge to Washington's G7 and even the
broader G20, because it includes the US. While it thus charts an
independent path, Beijing is at the same time using its alliances to
push for China and others to be allowed more influence in existing
international institutions like the UN, IMF, and the World Bank.[51]

FLASHPOINTS OF INTERIMPERIAL RIVALRY

While the US and China may strike temporary agreements like the
illusory climate change pact inked at COP26, these are unlikely to
establish any lasting cooperation between the two powers. There
are simply too many deep-rooted dynamics driving them toward
rivalry. Their intensifying competition will likely come to a head
in several points of sharp conflict. At the very foundation of the
rivalry—economics—they will likely find themselves in spiraling competition over trade; dueling development plans—BRI and
B3W—for the Global South; and especially high-tech and specifically semiconductors, both because of their centrality to the world
economy and because of their military applications.

This conflict has set in motion a logic of restructuring globalization, fragmenting the system into rival national security blocs
in some strategic economic areas while maintaining global supply
chains in others. This rivalry between the two states could lead
to a much deeper "blocification" of the world economy between
one centered on the US and another on China. But that would
entail multinational corporations abandoning enormous sums of
invested capital and intricate supply chains that have been central to the world economy. At this point, neither state is prepared
to force such segregation on its capitalist corporations. But each

is hedging against that possibility with their dueling industrial policies—Beijing's "dual circulation economy" and Washington's "de-risking strategy."

This underlying economic competition and tendency toward blocification will trigger increased geopolitical conflicts over spheres of influence. China will use its domestic market, BRI, and high-tech exports to expand its economic relations with states throughout the world, hoping to expand its geopolitical influence and number of international military bases. The US will counter, using both its even greater economic and financial power, especially the dollar as the global reserve currency, as well as its historic alliances, built over decades of imperial hegemony. Each will parlay their economic power to lure states into their orbit against the other.

Finally, and most ominously, the rivalry will trigger a struggle for military hegemony over the Asia Pacific and beyond. Already, the US and China have fueled an arms race in the region, with all states beefing up their defense budgets and military capacities to stake claims to islands, shipping lanes, fisheries, and undersea natural resources, especially fossil fuels. The US has escalated this with its ever-increasing deployment of its ships as well as those of its allies throughout the Asia Pacific. There have been numerous collisions and symbolic standoffs among various powers. This is a cauldron of potential conflict.

Of all the flashpoints, perhaps the most dangerous one is Taiwan. The battle among the powers over Taiwan is not just geopolitical, but also economic. China views Taiwan as part of its territory, Taiwan increasingly sees itself as an independent state, while the US views it as a means to push back against China's assertion of regional power. On top of that, Taiwan is the global center of advanced chip production, something as significant as oil to the world economy. Whoever has hegemony over Taiwan, therefore, has leverage over every single state and corporation in the world. Hence, the sharp standoff between the US and China. Lost amid this geopolitical jockeying has been Taiwan and its people's right to self-determination, free from the machinations of both imperialist powers.

MITIGATING TENDENCIES AGAINST IMPERIALIST WAR

Despite all these ominous signs, there are several dynamics particular to today's asymmetric multipolar world order that mitigate the tendency of interimperial rivalry to produce war between these two great powers. First and foremost, China and the US remain deeply tied together economically. That fosters capitalist and state interests on both sides against a descent into open confrontation. Any immediate decoupling is not on the table, despite the fact that trade between the two countries declined by 25 percent in 2023.[52] The US, as well as European and Japanese multinationals, use China to manufacture their products, and want more access to its enormous market, and Wall Street is eager to pursue opportunities there for financial investment. For now, China wants it that way. As a result, China remained the world's factory in 2023, churning out 31 percent of global manufacturing, nearly double that of the US, which ranked second at 17 percent.[53] At the same time, the growing economic, geopolitical, and military rivalry is undoubtedly driving a wedge between the two economies. But—absent the outbreak of war—any decoupling and blocification is likely to unfold over years, and not immediately.

Second, China remains weaker and unprepared to supplant the US from its dominant position. It is dependent on the US and its allies for high-tech research and design, especially in chips, and its currency cannot replace the dollar as the global reserve. Its military, while regionally strong, cannot match the US on a global scale. And geopolitically, its track record on the pandemic, human rights abuses, and mixed results on its BRI program has undercut its soft power. Therefore, it is likely to shrink back from direct confrontation, continuing to build its power to compete while it calls for cooperation. Third, this conflict is taking place in, around, and through an international architecture of interstate institutions set up and overseen by the US, like the WTO, the UN, the IMF, and the World Bank, as well as a host of economic and strategic pacts that crisscross and stabilize relations among the world's states. While these can dampen the tendency toward imperial war, they are at the same time in various stages of crisis in their functioning and legitimacy.

Finally, since both powers possess and are expanding nuclear arsenals, any military conflict could end in mutually assured destruction. Thus, in ways similar to the Cold War, it will push conflict to proxy battles in the system's periphery and into "geo-economic" competition, with each trying to carve out more clearly demarcated spheres of influence. These peculiar features of imperialism today mitigate the likelihood of war, but do not rule it out, including in the heartlands of the system, as the war in Ukraine and the conflict over Taiwan make abundantly clear. The system's long depression combined with increased economic and geopolitical blocification will drive each nation's ruling class toward nationalism to deflect blame for their problems onto the other. In these conditions, it would be a mistake to rule out the possibility that any of the growing number of conflicts could trigger an unintended and catastrophic military confrontation.

CHAPTER 7

CHINA AND GLOBAL CAPITALISM'S ECOLOGICAL AND CLIMATE CRISES

C apitalism's expansion has triggered global ecological and climate crises that pose an existential threat to humanity. Among
its many other consequences, the growing rivalry between the
US and China is preventing the development of collective international solutions to address these crises. Climate change is generating intense global heating, demonstrated by temperature records
being shattered in countries throughout the world, as well as by the
frequency of extreme weather. Overall, 2023 was the hottest year
yet, breaking the record of global heating set in 2016. Every other
year over the last decade is near those levels. The Intergovernmental Panel on Climate Change's Sixth Assessment Report ominously
warned that even with drastic cuts in greenhouse emissions today,
global temperature is still set to rise by around 1.5 degrees Celsius
within the next two decades.[1] This global heating is inducing ever
more severe weather patterns from record rainfalls to powerful hurricanes as well as droughts, desertification, and rising sea levels. All
of which are destabilizing societies and creating climate refugees
that join the already unprecedented waves of migrants fleeing the
depredations of global capitalism, state repression, and war. The

case is clear that nothing short of a radical transformation of our capitalist economies could avert ongoing catastrophe.

The United States and China are at the center of this climate crisis. The United States is historically the highest emitter and the current second-highest emitter, while China has become the highest emitter of CO2. China's rapid development as a new center of accumulation has significantly contributed to global emissions through its increasing demand for raw materials and funding of extractivist industries throughout the world. Rather than being a uniquely bad actor, however, China is following the same path as previous industrial powers, and one not separate from the rest of global capitalism, but an integral part of it. While China is not exceptional, the gigantic scale of its economic development is not only contributing significantly to climate change, but also other forms of environmental devastation in China and internationally, like soil erosion and desertification, as well as air and water pollution. To stop the system's wreckage of China and the global ecosphere will take more than the ineffectual international summits among the world's capitalist states. It will require an international movement of increasingly radical mass actions and climate strikes to force through programs like the Green New Deal on the road to a society that puts people and the planet first.

CHINA, GLOBAL CAPITALISM, AND CLIMATE CHANGE

The historical geography of environmental devastation and greenhouse gas emission is a story of global capitalist development. Industrialization in Western Europe was the earliest major source of emissions. Then by the middle of the twentieth century, the US surpassed Europe to become the leading emitter of CO2. Cumulatively, the US is more responsible than any other country for total greenhouse gasses. Only recently did China take the lead in emissions. A latecomer to industrialization and with that a sharp expansion of CO2 emission, China became the world's largest single emitter in 2006. By 2019, China's annual CO2 emissions were already double those of the US and accounted for 27 percent of the world's total, which was more than all developed economies combined, including the US at 11 percent.[2]

The rise of China's CO2 emissions has resulted in ecological disasters of historical proportions. This had already begun in the Mao era between 1949 and 1976, when the state invested in heavy industrialization to build up economic capacity and recover from decades of anti-colonial struggle and civil war. That development led to a surge in emissions from 59.27 million tons per year, at the start of the era, to 1.19 billion tons per year at its end. But in the post-Mao era China's emissions increased exponentially, reaching 10.17 billion tons per year in 2019.[3] This spike is a direct result of China's vast new capitalist development, industrialization, and urbanization that turned it from an underdeveloped agricultural society into a global economic powerhouse.

It would be misleading to see China's expansion as a purely domestic phenomenon. In fact, it has been fueled by global capitalism; foreign direct investment since the 1980s dramatically increased China's manufacturing capacity. Multinational corporations saw in China a spatial fix to restore their profitability. They took advantage of its cheap land and labor to build new plants to sell products in the country's huge domestic market, as well as export to the world market. At the same time, China was also a spatial fix for the advanced capitalist countries' ecological crisis. They relocated many of their "dirty industries" to China where environmental regulation was and is lax. China's capitalist industrial development transformed the country into the workshop of the world, the largest consumer of primary energy, the second-biggest consumer of fossil fuels (after the US), and the main source for global demand in industrial raw materials from the developing world. All of this has turned the country into global capitalism's epicenter of ecological disaster and global heating.

This capitalist development has generated a domestic and global ecological crisis centered in China with three main expressions: (1) the pollution of land, water and air, which has had a severe impact on the Chinese population but only a limited global impact; (2)

the emission of greenhouse gasses, which has a more limited immediate domestic impact but a monumental global impact; and (3) increased likelihood of epidemics and pandemics arising from environmental destruction and zoonotic spillover of animal viruses into the human population, which, with the emergence of COVID, has devastated global populations.

At the heart of the crisis is an economic developmental model based on fossil fuels. China followed the path blazed by the advanced capitalist states and economies. Coal is the source for over half of China's domestic energy. While various forms of clean energy are increasing quickly, they still only account for just a quarter of energy sources.[4] In 2020, China generated 53 percent of the world's total coal-fired power.[5] China Coal alone accounts for 14.32 percent of the total global emissions between 1988 and 2015, the highest among the one hundred firms responsible for over 70 percent of global emission over that period.[6] China is also the world's largest oil importer. In the last decade, China has imitated its advanced capitalist competitors, gradually displacing the epicenter of its ecological crisis onto other countries around the world. It has done this by cutting down some coal production within China and financing it elsewhere in the developing world through its Belt and Road Initiative. According to a 2021 report by the Beijing-based International Institute of Green Finance, more than 70 percent of all coal plants built in the world today rely on Chinese funding.[7] Its fossil-fuel reliant economic model drives extraction of coal, oil, and natural gas within China and internationally, generating $CO2$ emissions, climate change, global heating, and all their associated weather disasters.

CHINA'S RECORD ON THE CLIMATE CRISIS

To its credit, the Chinese government does not deny the existence of the climate crisis. It has openly recognized that human society drives climate change and stated explicitly the seriousness of the crisis. China ratified the Paris Climate Agreement in 2016 and since then Xi Jinping has been vocal in supporting global emission reductions and climate agreements. For instance, China announced in September 2020 that it will aim to hit peak emissions before 2030 and reach carbon neutrality by 2060. It later joined more than sixty other countries that have pledged carbon neutrality by 2050. Given China's dependence on fossil fuels, reaching such goals would be a significant achievement, but there are reasons to temper our optimism. After suffering widespread electricity shortages in 2021, the Chinese government increased coal production in 2022. China is locked into putting the pursuit of competitiveness, profitability, and growth before its environmental concerns.

China trumpets symbolic measures, enacts ineffectual schemes like carbon trading, but rejects systemic reforms that would address the crisis. Thus, at the Communist Party's 18th National Congress in 2012, a resolution was passed making "ecological civilization" one of China's core commitments and incorporating this into the constitution in 2018. Such measures have been forced on the state by popular expressions and protests from below. Over the last decade, mass discontent has developed over air pollution and other environmental problems. Chinese people have every reason to be angry. In a major study in the *Lancet*, it was estimated that 1.24 million deaths in China in 2017 could be attributed to air pollution.[8] Air pollution is just one of a host of environmental crises caused by the country's economic development, which include pollution of land and water, as well as increasing droughts, floods, and heatwaves. These all threaten people's lives and livelihoods and have produced many protests.

In some respects, China's response to the ecological crisis, popular discontent, and protest has been impressive. China has led the world in developing and producing renewable energy. In just 2020, it more than doubled its wind and solar power capacity. However, it is doing this while still maintaining and expanding its consumption of coal, which China deems essential to power its economy. As a result, even as it develops green sectors it has failed to reduce CO_2 emissions. The Chinese government has also pursued market-based solutions. In July 2021, China launched a national carbon market called the China Emissions Trading Scheme, the largest carbon market in the world. Yet researchers already point out that the initial carbon allowances are too generous, the prices for these allowances too low, and the penalties for failing to comply are not severe enough to be a deterrent. Like carbon markets elsewhere, they merely allow corporations to evade serious reform and find new ways to make money in trading the right to pollute.

CHINESE CHARACTERISTICS, OR CAPITALIST IMPERATIVE?

China's failure to adhere to its own promises, just like that of its global competitors, is structurally determined. Like all capitalist countries, it is subject to global capitalism's laws of competition for the sake of profit and growth, as well as its crises of overaccumulation, overproduction, and profitability. On top of this, the Chinese state's very legitimacy in the eyes of its workers hinges on its ability to guarantee growth and the promise of improved standards of living. To explain the causes of China's ecological crisis, some argue that China is not governed simply by a capitalist logic of accumulation, but instead is a bureaucratic collectivist society, whose state's irrational priority of self-preservation above all else makes it more prone to environmental devastation and less responsive to popular pressure than Western liberal democracies.[9] Others contend that China is a socialist society with state ownership of important parts of the economy, which makes it more adept than capitalist societies in undertaking large-scale, state-coordinated actions to enact reforms to address climate change.

It is true that the dictatorial nature of the Chinese state makes it harder for the public to express discontent through street demonstrations, form advocacy groups, and impact state policies. This lack of democracy notwithstanding, it is not true that popular pressure and struggle has no impact on state policy. In fact, popular discontent and resistance has forced the state to enact measures that at least partially address environmental degradation. For instance, popular criticism by urban residents against air pollution in major cities like Beijing pushed the government to shut down or relocate highly polluting industries. It is also true that the Chinese state maintains ownership and control over substantial sections of the economy, implements forms of industrial planning, and disciplines some sections of private capital. But, as has been argued, the state, its SOEs, and private capital are driven by global capitalism's laws of competition, and do not make the system socialist.

Both positions ultimately mirror each other in arguing that China has unique, noncapitalist characteristics, with one merely saying that those are negative and with the other claiming the opposite. Despite its particular history, China's state and economy are thoroughly integrated into global capitalism and its interstate system. As a result, it is following the well-trodden path of capitalist industrialization that other wealthy economies have undertaken, and it is addressing the climate crisis just like other capitalist states, through regulation, incentives, the development of renewable energy, improved efficiency, and a carbon market, all while it continues to use increasing amounts of fossil fuels. It views its successful development of renewables not primarily as a means to reduce carbon emissions, but as an opportunity to corner those markets and make windfall profits. Thus, China is not separate and apart from the rest of global capitalism, but an integral part of it, including its climate crisis.

THE GLOBAL CAPITALIST CLIMATE CRISIS

Any possibility of addressing the climate crisis depends on what China and the US do. While Europe and the US have historically been the main drivers of climate change, China has now supplanted them, and its emissions have to be curtailed in order to avoid ecological catastrophe. In recognizing this, it is important to underscore that China is not exceptional, but that it is a key part of a global problem and what it does or does not do will determine whether climate change is mitigated. Indeed, China is the best illustration of how the crisis is a product not of this or that nation but global capitalism itself.

As foreign direct investment (FDI) pours into China and Chinese companies, global emissions get logged as Chinese emissions. It is at the heart of the world economy and its supply chains, proving that the associated emissions are not "Chinese" but, in fact, those of global capitalism and its integrated economies. Seeing the ecological crisis in national terms—as American, European, or Chinese—prevents us from seeing the global nature of the problem and obstructs building an international movement for climate justice and system change. Demanding that China, or the US, or any other country radically reduce emissions is necessarily part of a struggle for the transformation of global capitalism into an ecological sustainable society and economy.

That transformation requires a challenge to the policies and priorities of all the dominant capitalist states, including China's. The climate justice movement faces real systemic obstacles in getting China and the other capitalist powers to implement system reforms to address the climate crisis. China and the US are locked in global competition that makes cooperation on climate change very difficult, because any serious changes will require fundamental economic changes, something both fear will compromise their position in the world system. As a result, nothing less than an international mass movement will be required to force them to enact meaningful reform.

CHINESE ENVIRONMENTAL STRUGGLES

Domestic activism in China will be a key part of this global struggle. The country's environmental movement has been led by spontaneous acts of popular protests and dedicated environmental NGOs. The increased space in civil society since the 1990s enabled both Chinese and international environmental groups to open offices and advocate for better regulations. Such environmental activism, like their counterparts in feminist and labor NGOs, has recently been restrained by the state, but it still has more space for its advocacy than labor and feminist activism because it is seen less as a political and politicized issue than the others. But without mass pressure from below they have not been able to win significant change.

For its part, the Chinese state wants to convey that it is enacting all the reforms that are necessary and has gone out of its way to contain and co-opt the struggle from below. The government's hope is to promote the role of individual responsibility as the mechanism to lessen each person's carbon footprint. Such individualist environmentalism, very familiar to people all around the world, is taught in Chinese schools. While it recognizes that climate change is a real problem and product of human society, its prescription that taking personal responsibility—without structural changes to energy consumption—will solve the crisis is a fantasy. This prevents the emergence of a serious movement that could challenge the capitalist system it oversees.

But there are signs that indicate the potential for more structurally focused struggles to develop. Inspired by Greta Thunberg, Howey Ou and Nlocy Jiang, two young Chinese high school students, staged their own climate strike and protest. It is not surprising that young people, who more than anyone else will bear the consequences of the climate crisis, were spurred into action. They faced immediate harassment by the authorities. The two activists were not backed by any existing groups, nor did their actions trigger the emergence of a large-scale movement. Their resistance remained acts of heroic individuals, but they are not alone. They are an expression of the growing consciousness among regular people about the looming crisis. Public opinion polls have shown that the Chinese public is increasingly concerned about the environment and climate crisis.[10] People rank the environment as a major concern even before education, economic development, and anti-terrorism. They also are willing to pay more for environmental and climate-friendly products and to make major adjustments of lifestyles. They also strongly support the government taking more responsibility in tackling climate change, with the majority strongly supporting stronger domestic policies and international cooperation.

This consciousness has been expressed dramatically in local, collective struggles against toxic incinerators and chemical plants in cities across the country. Typically, these are massive urban street demonstrations, which last for days and tend to end up winning their key demands. While this is good for the local community, these movements generally dissipate as quickly as they came together. They are often labeled as NIMBY (Not In My Back Yard) protests that ultimately just relocate rather than fundamentally address the environmental crisis. But such criticism is not fair. In fact, such struggles have radical potential; they are examples of ordinary people exercising their power against corporations, winning their demands, and building their confidence to demand more. If these localized battles can be knitted together in a common struggle for shared demands, they could form the basis of a mass environmental movement necessary to force the Chinese state to enact serious reforms.

Mass movements are needed because the transformations will need to be radical, democratic, and international in nature. The global climate strikes offer a glimpse of the kind of movement that will be necessary to compel individual states and, indeed, all of them to implement drastic changes. In a perverse manner, the COVID pandemic shows what states can do when faced with an emergency. It provides a glimpse of the kind of drastic mobilization of resources and personnel, and global collaboration—uneven and contradictory as that was—to address a crisis that will be needed to stop global heating. For a brief moment in early 2020, when governments around the world imposed lockdowns, emissions dropped dramatically. In China, air pollution dissipated when industry shut down. Globally, emissions dipped sharply in the first few months by 6.4 percent, or 2.3 billion tons, before rebounding.[11] This is a significant reduction in such a short period of time, and shows such reduction is possible if needed.

The problem was that countries saw this as temporary, had no plans for converting the system, and restarted business as usual as quickly as possible regardless of the risk to life and damage to the environment. Nonetheless, the pandemic demonstrated that faced with an emergency, governments can take radical measures to overcome a crisis. Global climate change is just such a crisis, but the capitalist states are so deeply entrenched in the fossil fuel economy that they will not act and certainly won't make changes that cut into their profit margins and competitive capacity against their state rivals. The challenge, then, for climate justice activists is to build an international movement that connects all the local grievances, from China to the US and throughout the world, especially in the Global South, and uses mass struggle to shut down business as usual and force governments to adopt our program of radical reforms like the Green New Deal on the road to much more far-reaching systemic change.

CHAPTER 8

PANDEMICS IN AN EPOCH OF IMPERIAL RIVALRY

In contrast to their response to climate change, most states took unprecedented emergency measures in reaction to the COVID pandemic. But profound divisions among them, most importantly between China and the US, prevented a coherent global response, especially to address the virus's sweep through the Global South. The pandemic broke out in China at a high point of the developing interimperial rivalry between Beijing and Washington toward the end of Trump's term as president. Both powers used the crisis to advance their geopolitical interests, the US working to shore up its global dominance and China flexing its muscle as an emerging power. While each deflected blame for the crisis on the other, the truth is that both share culpability for the COVID catastrophe. They are both expanding, overseeing, and enforcing global capitalism's encroachment on previously isolated ecosystems, which enable viruses to jump from animals to humans. Once an epidemic breaks out in one country, it can quickly spread through the world's integrated system of production and infect people from Wuhan to Washington. Thus, the age of capitalist globalization is also the age of pandemics.

While the US, China, and other imperialist states oversee this system, they also compete for dominance within it. They are, as Marx said, a band of warring brothers. So, when COVID struck, the rivalry between the US and China and its reverberations throughout the state system blocked meaningful international collaboration in forging a joint plan to manage the global health crisis. Instead, the dominant states in Western Europe and North America put their own national, economic, and geopolitical interests first. Even then, they all failed the test of the pandemic. China suppressed news of the outbreak, allowed the virus to spread inside China and beyond its borders, and only took decisive actions when forced from below by whistleblowers and activists. It then mobilized its state power to shut down the country, suppress the virus, and quickly reopen business to get profit flowing again.

It tried to capitalize on its success, whipping up nationalism domestically, promoting conspiracy theories about how the virus originated outside of China, suppressing dissent that questioned the official narrative, and cultivating old and new alliances abroad through vaccine diplomacy to repair the damage to its image from the initial outbreak. The emergence of the omicron variant threw this initial success into crisis. Faced with the spread of the virus, China intensified its zero-COVID policy, imposing brutal lockdowns on entire cities and regions. These harsh measures disrupted global supply chains and tarnished Beijing's reputation. The state only abandoned this policy when faced with mass strikes and protests, combined with outbreaks it was failing to control. Like other states in the world, it recklessly reopened society without any clear plans and measures in place to protect its population, which suffered an unprecedented wave of infections and untold numbers of deaths.

The US also completely bungled its response to COVID, ensuring that it became the epicenter of the pandemic. While the Trump administration funded the vaccine research, it stooped to new racist lows, blaming China for the pandemic while it did little to stop its lethal spread throughout the US, politicized shutdowns as an infringement on individual liberty, setting the stage for mass refusal of the vaccines, which was the only breakthrough the US made in fighting the pandemic. While the Biden administration replaced anti-scientific lunacy with rational policy, it engaged in its own "America First" policy, hoarding vaccines until public pressure finally forced it to distribute them in the Global South. It then turned that to its advantage, in its own version of pandemic diplomacy. Like other states, the Biden administration normalized the pandemic and suspended any and all precautions. At the same time, it intensified the conflict with China over everything from trade to semiconductors and COVID itself. Thus, the pandemic has accentuated the interimperial rivalry, limiting chances for collaboration on this epidemiological crisis and future ones.

THE ORIGINS OF THE PANDEMIC

While there is no doubt that the virus first emerged in China, its origins remain unclear. Most scientists suspect it was the result of zoonotic spillover, most likely from bats via animals like the pangolin sold in the wet market in Wuhan. Others, including some US intelligence agencies, allege, based on scant evidence, that COVID's emergence was the result of an accident at the Wuhan Institute of Virology, which has had outbreaks in the past. While the virus's exact origins remain scientifically undetermined, it is entirely mistaken to single out China as uniquely to blame. In fact, epidemiologists have been warning about the possibility of a pandemic breaking out anywhere in the world. They saw the 2002 SARS epidemic in China, the 2009 H1N1 "swine flu" in the US, and West Africa's 2014 ebola outbreak as early signs of the growing likelihood of a pandemic. In September 2019, just a few months before the COVID-19 outbreak, *The World at Risk* report produced by the Global Preparedness Monitoring Board, an independent group of experts convened by the World Bank and the World Health Organization (WHO), warned:

> While disease has always been part of the human experience, a combination of global trends, including insecurity and extreme weather, has heightened the risk. Disease thrives in disorder and has taken advantage—outbreaks have been on the rise for the past several decades and the specter of a global health emer-

gency looms large . . . there is a very real threat of a rapidly mov-
ing, highly lethal pandemic of a respiratory pathogen killing
50 to 80 million people and wiping out nearly 5 percent of the
world's economy. A global pandemic on that scale would be catastrophic, creating widespread havoc, instability, and insecurity.
The world is not prepared.[1]

Neoliberal capitalism, with its profit-driven destruction of natural
habitats, relentless evisceration of state services, and gutting of public health care systems, set the stage not only for pandemics but for
them to lead to mass sickness and death. International agribusiness
holds particular responsibility; it has cut down the world's forests
to build factory farms near heretofore isolated ecosystems. These
farms enable the passage of pathogens from wildlife to domesti-
cated animals and then to humans. And, once epidemics break out
anywhere, their viruses can quickly travel through global capitalism's integrated system of production, supply, distribution, and sale
to infect the world.

The threat of such pandemics has compelled states, universities, and corporations to construct high-tech labs to study the
world's most dangerous viruses, in the hopes of devising vaccines
to cure them. These have proliferated throughout the world in
the last few decades.[2] In turn, they become potential sites for accidents that could leak old and new viruses, triggering the very
pandemics they are designed to prevent. Of course, such accidents
are extremely rare, and the overwhelming majority of epidemics
are the result of zoonotic spillover. But they have happened in
various countries and should be reason enough for the world's
states to cooperate with one another and ramp up regulation and
safety procedures to prevent outbreaks from labs. But, again, a
combination of deregulation and interstate rivalry has impeded
such rational policy. As Dhruv Khullar reports, "Globally there is
no comprehensive inventory, let alone rigorous oversight, of laboratories that handle highly contagious and deadly pathogens; in
the U.S., the lab-safety system is 'a total crazy patchwork quilt of
rules,' a scientist told the *Times*'s David Wallace-Wells. It's not
always clear who's responsible for ensuring that a lab adheres to

safety protocols, or even what those protocols should be."[3] This frightening reality underscores the point that China is part of a much larger problem of lax regulation of such necessary but potentially dangerous research, a problem in which the US and many other states are implicated.

Once pathogens break out, whether from zoonotic spillover or rare lab leaks, most states, including advanced capitalist ones, are ill-prepared to manage them. Neoliberal policies have eviscerated welfare states around the world, making it very hard for governments to stop pandemics or treat those who fall sick. Thus, the system and all its states are the problem, not any particular state. It's important to reject explanations that solely blame China for COVID because they divert attention away from the systemic roots of recent pandemics and the role of global capitalism in creating and spreading them with more frequency. The coronavirus could have emerged elsewhere. The fact that it did emerge in China is not the result of anything unique to Chinese people or culture, but the globally driven, rapid development of Chinese capitalism as the workshop of the world.

That said, we can see how the international pattern of corporate encroachment on isolated ecosystems has been concentrated and accelerated in China. Its unprecedented economic expansion over the last forty years has led to breakneck urbanization, including the building of whole new cities out of small towns, and massive development of commercial agriculture in the countryside. This has been a state-led economic strategy to boost consumption, as China tries to shift away from export dependency. All this development has caused significant deterioration in 90 percent of China's grasslands and 40 percent of its wetlands, threatening species with extinction and eroding biodiversity.[4]

On top of this, the Chinese state has for years encouraged poor farmers to increase their incomes by culling exotic animals from isolated ecosystems, with their pathogens, and selling them mostly to the rich and professional middle class. This is a nightmare scenario for zoonotic spillover. Of course, such exterminationist trafficking in endangered wildlife for consumption and sport is an international phenomenon, and one engaged in by the US elite. But that is no alibi for the Chinese state. After the dangers of this market in exotic animals enabling the transmission of pathogens into humans became clear, China rushed to contain it, but the lucrative business continues and will take years to eradicate. China's urbanization, industrialization, intense expansion of agribusiness, and capitalization of exotic species are a recipe for epidemics. Its lax regulation of its laboratories set up to research and prevent outbreaks, like that of SARS, and refusal to cooperate with other states only compounds the danger. As we've seen, the country's deep integration into the world economy means that what happens in China cannot stay in China. It will spread at the pace of just-in-time production along the supply chains of global capitalism. So, once COVID emerged in China, its epidemic became a pandemic throughout the world in just a couple of months.

THE MYTH OF CHINESE EXCEPTIONALISM

While most of the world was gripped by the pandemic in 2020 and 2021, China successfully suppressed the virus within its borders by May 2020 until the emergence of the omicron variant in late 2021. Before then, it imposed unprecedented lockdowns, elaborate digital surveillance, and mass quarantines of infected people to isolate the virus, stop its spread, and largely eliminate it in the country. Initially these draconian measures were condemned, but with their success, China managed to transform itself from the global scapegoat for the pandemic to a model in how to suppress it. The government's account of its success is at odds with reality. Like almost every state in the world, China fumbled its response to the pandemic. It initially suppressed information during the first outbreak in Wuhan. The local government had known that the virus had been circulating in early December 2019, but, out of a combination of fear of its superiors and incompetence, blocked it being reported to the Chinese Center for Disease Control (CCDC), which was set up to monitor such dangers after China's complete failure to respond to the SARS outbreak in 2003. It even forced Dr. Li Wenliang, who had shared news of the outbreak with other doctors, to confess the crime of spreading false information.

Even when the CCDC found out about the human-to-human transmission, it did not alert the public, nor the WHO.[5] China's National Health Commission denied the fact of transmission throughout January 2020. It went so far as to prohibit the publication of laboratory findings about the nature of the virus and its spread. Even when the reality of the crisis was undeniable later in January, Xi gave a speech in which he did not even mention human-to-human transmission, despite it sweeping through Wuhan. China even lobbied against the WHO, declaring a "Public Health Emergency of International Concern." Xi did not want to interfere with China's Lunar New Year festivities.

It took heroic actions by health professionals, scientists, and workers to force the state to respond. Doctors like Li, who lost his life to COVID, defied the authorities to expose the emergency.[6] And people turned to social media to express concern. That forced the government to finally act, ordering the quarantining of Wuhan and announcing a state-led "people's war" to suppress the spread of the virus. But he launched this effort far too late, giving nearly two months for the virus to spread within and beyond China to the rest of the world. While the state declared a people's war and shut down China, the people themselves played an even more significant role in overcoming the crisis. In Wuhan, volunteers organized delivery of medical supplies and other necessities and provided volunteer transportation of medical workers to and from work. Across China, popularly organized groups monitored people's health. And, in defiance of the government, a small group of activists launched a public campaign to stop workers from returning to work after their Lunar New Year holidays. They organized a mass social media campaign, attracting millions of views online.

Student volunteers, concerned with the lack of protection for sanitation workers, organized a campaign to draw public attention.

Spreading across more than a dozen cities in China, hundreds of volunteers tried to monitor the situation of sanitation workers and donated masks and other personal protective equipment (PPE). This was followed by more organized, as well as spontaneous, campaigns for donations of PPE. Independent labor groups, already under sustained political attacks for years, provided legal advice to workers facing factory shutdowns, donated masks and gloves to workers, and launched online support networks for them. Others campaigned to reduce rent for workers, and to have domestic workers paid while in quarantine. Feminist activists organized to shine a light on increased domestic violence during lockdowns, and others drew attention to the lack of female hygiene products among frontline medical workers and called for donations.

These are just a few examples of the vast self-mobilization of ordinary people and grassroots groups for their self-protection and mutual aid.[7] Mass popular mobilization ensured the safety and well-being of people and their society when the state failed to provide such protection. These mobilizations played a decisive role in solving people's problems, overcoming the difficulties of life under quarantine, and providing collective care in the early months of the outbreak in China.

FROM REPRESSION AND ZERO-COVID TO UNIVERSAL COVID

Meanwhile, the state was most concerned to quash the dissent that this popular mobilization unleashed. They did not want their scandalous failure to stop the virus exposed. They disciplined Dr. Li for going public, exposing his censure, and even for revealing that he tested positive for COVID. He became a public hero for resistance to the state, inspiring people to demand greater freedom. In the hours after his death, over two million people shared the hashtag #Iwantfreedomofspeech.

That was only one example of repression. The state also disappeared Fang Bin, a worker in a clothing shop, for posting videos exposing images of the sick and dead in Wuhan and for calling on the "people to revolt" and "hand the power of the government back to the people." A human rights lawyer, Chen Qiushi, similarly disappeared after he released a YouTube video to his four hundred thousand followers promising to expose what was actually happening in Wuhan. The authorities were so worried about dissent that they increased their already draconian control over the internet. As part of that effort, they arrested several programmers that worked for a GitHub initiative called Terminus 2049 that aimed to preserve digital records about the outbreak from being erased. The state itself admitted that it has punished some 897 people for the crime of "spreading rumors." No doubt the actual number was much, much higher.

Thus, the pandemic exposed not the greater capacity of the Chinese state, but its bureaucratic inertia, paranoia, and incapacity to respond to the crisis except through repression. As the radical journal *Chuang* argues, the state response demonstrates "the repressive capacity of the Chinese state, but it also emphasizes the deeper incapacity of that state, revealed by its need to rely so heavily on a combination of total propaganda measures deployed through every facet of the media and the goodwill mobilizations of locals otherwise under no material obligation to comply."[8] The state put its public image over and above the health of its citizens and that of the world's population. That brought it into deep disrepute from the states of the world and from its own people. However, as the unfolding events have proved, the prediction of the imminent collapse of the CCP was also overblown. The state managed to pull through the crisis and whip up nationalism to trumpet its "success" even as it doubled down on repression within its borders.

Part of its repressive response to the pandemic was its policy of Zero-COVID, which barred travel in and out of the country and reacted harshly to any sign of the virus emerging. In response to any positive tests and especially omicron outbreak, the government imposed severe lockdowns to isolate and contain the virus's spread. These were of a different nature than lockdowns in other parts of the world. They trapped people in their apartments and deprived them of access to adequate food and health care for days, weeks, and even months on end. Increasingly, people began to complain about the repressive nature of these lockdowns, expressing outrage particularly against the government employees enforcing them. While zero-COVID in combination with vaccination worked for a time in keeping the virus under control, the lockdowns threatened to disrupt production. To avoid this, companies adopted "closed-loop management," forcing workers to live at their workplaces.[9] But it proved impossible to completely isolate workplaces from the rest of society and block the virus from getting in and infecting workers trapped in factories.

It was only a matter of time before this combustible situation exploded. Workers rose up against "closed-loop management" in violent strikes at Foxconn's massive iPhone factory in Zhengzhou. Then when a horrific fire in an apartment complex under lockdown in Ürümqi, the capital of Xinjiang, killed and injured many people, almost all Uyghurs, activists organized unprecedented protests throughout the country, demanding the end of Zero-COVID. Chinese overseas students organized protests in countries throughout the world. Not only had Zero-COVID triggered protest, but it was no longer even stopping the spread of the virulent omicron virus. Hoping to quell mass resistance, the government suddenly reversed course, abandoned Zero-COVID for "universal COVID," opened up the country without proper preparations, and let the virus rip through society, infecting and killing untold numbers of people, disproportionately old and unvaccinated. The state, however, trumpeted its decision, especially its opening up to the rest of the world in order to get its economy up and running.

IMPERIAL RIVALRY IN THE TIME OF PANDEMICS

During the pandemic, China became even more assertive, exerting both its soft and hard power. It used its successful creation of the Sinovac-CoronaVac and Sinopharm vaccines to rebuild its reputation internationally. It shared its vaccine with allies and with countries it sought to woo into its orbit and cultivated the myth of the superiority of its response to the pandemic. At the same time, China adopted an even more belligerent posture in its Asian sphere of influence, ratcheting up military pressure on Taiwan in particular in response to US provocations.

For its part, Washington used the pandemic to shore up its dominance as the global hegemon and contain China's challenge to its rule. The Trump administration botched Washington's initial response to the COVID emergency. Worried that any shutdown of the economy would harm his chances of reelection, Trump overruled his advisors clamoring for a response, siding with others counseling a wait-and-see approach to the outbreak, preventing the implementation of any rational, national policy to the rapidly spreading virus. He gambled everything on the virus burning itself out and the introduction of a vaccine to salvage his campaign for reelection.

With that looking highly unlikely and the bodies piling up in morgues around the country, Trump finally ordered the closure of US borders and a national shutdown to stop the spread of the virus. While he kept the borders closed to advance his xenophobic anti-immigrant agenda, he shifted into opposition to shutdowns to get the economy up and running as quickly as possible. Even worse, he politicized health policies like mask and vaccine requirements as infringements on individual liberties. That ensured that his far-right base would rally against rational measures to stop the spread of the virus, guaranteeing low rates of vaccination in whole swaths of the country that eventually turned the US into the epicenter of the pandemic.

With his administration reeling, Trump stooped to racist, xenophobic attacks against China to deflect attention from his responsibility for the catastrophe in the US. He insisted on calling COVID "the China Virus" and "Kung Flu" even at the cost of blocking an international agreement on pandemic policy from the G7, which refused to use the term in their official documents. Trump also ratcheted up attacks on Chinese scientists at American universities, leading to their surveillance and interrogation. Amid this anti-Chinese turn from the federal government, the US saw a sharp spike in violence not only against Chinese and Chinese Americans, but all Asians in the country. Doomed to defeat by the pandemic and recession, Trump left office having ratcheted up the conflict with Beijing to an unprecedented level of hostility. While his successor Joe Biden stripped China policy of its explicit racism, he stuck to the imperial consensus in Washington that China is a great power rival that must be enticed, bullied, and disciplined into accepting US hegemony over the world order. In pursuit of this, Biden, like Trump, weaponized the pandemic. He pushed for investigation of the Wuhan Institute of Virology based on the suspect "lab leak" theory of COVID's origins.

Rather than bringing the US and China, as well as the rest of the world's states, together to overcome a global health emergency, the pandemic has sharpened antagonisms among all of them. The pandemic became the occasion for nationalist solutions among all capitalist states to global capitalism's multiplying crises, from the pandemic and the recession it triggered to the uninterrupted march of climate change and the endless environmental catastrophes it entailed—from desertification to unprecedented hurricanes to gigantic wildfires. More than any other crisis, the pandemic exposed the incapacity of the world's key rival powers, the US and China, to address any of these crises ravaging people's lives. The virus continues to sweep across the world, leaving at least four million people dead in its wake, tens of millions sickened, and growing numbers plagued by long COVID.

PART IV

INTERNATIONAL SOLIDARITY
FROM BELOW

CHAPTER 9

"CHINA" IN THE US

The Roots and Nature of Diasporic Struggles

We have little choice but to build solidarity across borders against imperial rivalry between the US and China and to seek out systemic solutions to global capitalism's multiple crises. Within the US, there are many opportunities to organize such solidarity from below between the two societies. In reality, China is not separate and apart from the US. Not only are the two economies deeply integrated, so are its people. In the US, there are large numbers of Chinese Americans and Chinese nationals, especially Chinese international students, whose numbers have exceeded three hundred thousand. They form a growing percentage of the Asian American population, a community that has never been passive, and their struggles are an important starting point for building solidarity.

Asian Americans organized to resist the racism Trump whipped up to deflect blame for the pandemic onto China, and, by extension, Chinese people and Chinese Americans. As COVID swept across the United States, Chinese and other Asian Americans became the target of assaults around the country. Between March 2020 and September 2021, more than ten thousand anti-Asian hate incidents such as verbal harassment, refusal of service at a business, online abuse, physical assaults, and property damage had been reported, according to the Asian American–Pacific Islander Equity

Alliance.[1] Asian Americans built on a legacy of social resistance in bringing attention to, and fighting back against, these acts of racism and xenophobia.

The anti-Asian racism did not originate with the pandemic, but has deep roots in US history going back to the Chinese Exclusion Act at the end of the nineteenth century. It has always been whipped up by the establishment to justify Washington's imperialist projects—whatever those may be at the time—and to disrupt workers' solidarity. Even before the pandemic, Trump scapegoated China for the predicament facing US workers, instituted policies to racially profile Chinese Americans, and thereby triggered increased bigotry against Asian Americans that reached fever pitch during the pandemic. Thus, US imperialism in Asia breeds anti-Asian racism at home. The resistance of Asian Americans (especially that of Chinese Americans) and the Chinese nationals in the US should be a central component of our efforts to build solidarity from below against the domestic and international divisions stoked by the US-China rivalry.

MIGRATION, RACISM, AND RESISTANCE

To be sure, Asian Americans are not and have never been a monolith. The group comprises multiple nationalities arriving in successive waves of migration from Asia from the mid-nineteenth century onward.[2] Despite the stereotype that East Asians are an economically privileged "model minority," their history, especially that of Chinese immigrants, over the past two centuries is rife with oppression and exploitation as well as resistance. Their presence in the US is a product of Washington's imperialist policies in Asia over the last century and a half. That history, combined with the US's current rivalry with Beijing are the backdrop to the emergence of a new generation of Chinese American activists and their organizing work today.

In the nineteenth century, the US attracted its first wave of Asian immigrants. These were impoverished Chinese men who left their hometowns amid economic decline and political instability during the late Qing dynasty. In the US, they found poorly paid jobs in agriculture, mining, and railway construction, and endured discrimination and terrible conditions at work with little social or political support. Against such treatment, Chinese workers organized and fought for better pay, benefits, and work rules. In June 1867, angered by the dangerous working conditions and discrimination in pay, Chinese railway workers, who had been building the transcontinental railroad, downed their tools and staged a historic eight-day strike for equal pay, shorter working hours, and better working conditions.[3] The employers responded by stoking racism and division among workers. These efforts led to a rising tide of anti-Asian bigotry that was turned into official state policy through successive discriminatory immigration laws, finally culminating in the Chinese Exclusion Act of 1882, a law that banned all Chinese immigration to the US. Despite this repression, Chinatowns continued to organize against racism and to offer a space for mutual aid.

The next major wave of Asian immigration came during the 1960s amid the Cold War. Unlike earlier migrants who were mostly poor and working class, the new immigrants were from relatively privileged backgrounds. This change was a direct result of US policy, as the Hart-Celler Act of 1965 opened the door to non-Europeans and gave preferential treatment for highly educated workers and middle-class professionals. This policy formed the basis of the "model minority" myth. Despite their professional background, these new immigrants faced racism and employment discrimination that made it hard to use their qualifications to find jobs in the US comparable to the ones they had in their homelands. Most of the Asian migrants came from countries aligned with Washington in the Cold War, such as South Korea, Taiwan, Hong Kong, the Philippines, and South Vietnam. Many of these immigrants harbored anti-communist views based on their experiences under regimes in their countries. Given the tense political relations with the US, migration from mainland China during the Mao era was all but impossible.

This second wave of Asian immigration coincided with the anti-war and Civil Rights movements in the US. Many second- and third-generation Asian Americans participated in and built alliances with these movements and became political radicals in the process. Some worked closely with and were inspired by the Black Panther Party, and others set up their own revolutionary organizations such as I Wor Kuen to engage in radical anti-racist, anti-capitalist, and anti-imperialist struggles. This activism forged the category "Asian American" as more than a description of racial identities, but a slogan of a radical, and in some cases revolution- ary, project aiming to build a movement of progressive Asians in the US. These struggles took on an array of forms. Some defended Asian communities from gentrification and eviction, and others coalesced around the Third World Liberation Front, which fought for, and eventually won, the creation of ethnic studies programs at universities whose research centered on Asian American commu- nities. Despite dissipating by the late 1970s, this militancy left a legacy of community organizations that continue to defend Asian American communities today.

CHINESE INTERNATIONAL STUDENTS

After the resumption of diplomatic relations between the US and China in the 1970s, students from China, usually sponsored by the Chinese government, began to arrive in the US, at first in small numbers for graduate study. China's democracy movement in 1989 and its aftermath had a profound impact on this era of US-China relations. College students and workers in China par- ticipated in large numbers in the movement but were met with harsh repression at the hands of the state. Many student leaders fled or were forced into exile in the West. The dissidents, who were still mostly in their twenties at the time, tried to build a dissident community and sustain their activism in exile. But their detachment from struggles on the ground in China, their failure to relate to any progressive social movements in the US, and their incessant factional infighting, ultimately made much of their activism ineffective.

While many of the dissident exiles described themselves as "liberals" in the Chinese context, some aligned themselves with anti-communist, right-wing political forces in the US, and morphed into neoliberals and neoconservatives. This pattern has continued to the present day, with some more recently exiled dissidents becoming pro-Trump and adopting the contemporary conservative political agenda.[4] As a result, there is an organized Chinese right in the US. Other exiles have refused the lure of right-wing anti-communism. Often these individuals are labor and feminist activists, whose political commitments bring them into opposition to the right's pro-capitalist and misogynist politics. Many of today's Chinese students—like the majority of other students—do not have clearly defined political views. Nevertheless, some of them have joined social movements from Black Lives Matter to graduate workers' unionization campaigns.

This most recent wave of students and immigrants was, until recently, shaped by the honeymoon period between Washington and Beijing after China joined the WTO in 2001. While the US developed a large trade deficit in industrial products with China,[5] it enjoyed a trade surplus in services, one key part of which has been higher education. In 2019, US exports in education totaled roughly $44 billion, making education the sixth-largest service export that year.[6] Chinese students have made up the largest portion of foreign students in the US. These students and young professionals from China are creating a new Chinese diaspora.[7]

Chinese students have become vital to the survival of American higher education in the neoliberal period. As a result of severe cuts in state funding, public universities have to reduce the number of enrollment slots for in-state applicants and expand their overseas market, targeting full-tuition-paying undergraduate and graduate students from rising middle-income countries. Deemed the cash cow, Chinese students, 40 percent of whom are undergrads, contributed $15 billion to the US economy in 2018 alone.[8] The Chinese state has organized Confucius Institutes on

US campuses to provide support and language instruction for students, while controversially maintaining control over curriculum and hiring decisions. The US state has treated these institutes with suspicion, while underprivileged communities have sometimes embraced them because funding cuts have deprived them of language programs.

While American universities have been welcoming of Chinese students over the last two decades, they have now become a key battleground in the US-China rivalry. The Trump-era China Initiative is emblematic of this conflict spilling onto American campuses. The Trump administration's stated aim was to investigate and prosecute researchers based at US universities who stole and shared cutting-edge technologies with China. In reality, the program racially profiled Chinese and Chinese American students and researchers simply because of their nationality or ethnicity, destroying several lives and careers in the process. Apart from whipping up racism, it has proved remarkably ineffective in accomplishing its stated goals.[9] What it has achieved is to create an atmosphere of fear of collaboration between US academics and their Chinese counterparts, damaging scientific research in the process.[10]

The Biden administration terminated the China Initiative in February 2022 and replaced it with a new and more comprehensive policy that targets a wider range of academics and researchers, effectively continuing the same surveillance minus the overt racial profiling. The Chinese state has long maintained similar suspicion of foreign collaboration. It has subjected academics in China who collaborate with international, and especially "Western," research institutions and colleagues to close political scrutiny. Especially in the humanities and social sciences, collaboration with foreign academics is a risky endeavor for Chinese scholars. The result is that students and academics in both countries are caught in the imperial rivalry and find themselves increasingly under siege.

The US mainstream media has tended to portray the new generation of Chinese students as national chauvinists indulging in conspicuous consumption. This is a distorted picture to say the least. In reality, Chinese students on US campuses are quite diverse socioeconomically and politically. While quite a few Chinese students are from well-off backgrounds and can even afford private boarding schools, many are from humble origins without significant wealth. According to the "White Paper on Chinese Students Studying Abroad 2021,"[11] about 40 percent of the students have parents who hold rank-and-file "white-collar" jobs. This is in contrast to their composition just a decade ago, when most students came from families of higher socioeconomic status. Today's less affluent families that send their children to school in the US often have to sell their apartments or even put themselves in debt. These families are willing to make such sacrifices and pay exorbitant tuition at US universities to give their children opportunities that lesser quality universities in China would not offer them. For these students, getting a degree in business or engineering is not only a way for them to get a decent education and to open the possibility of their own class advancement, but also a way to improve their families' lives and incomes.[12]

In addition to socioeconomic differences, Chinese students are further separated by program of study. While most of them were in business management, math and hard science, and engineering—feeding into the stereotype that Chinese students are only good at STEM and not interested in politics—a small portion (10 percent) are in social sciences and humanities.[13] Despite their small numbers, this group plays a crucial role in shaping the discourse among Chinese students, as students pursuing a major or postgraduate degree in social sciences or humanities tend to have a more critical view of the world, including the Chinese government. Enrolling in seminars on modern Chinese history, comparative politics, social inequalities in Chinese society, to give a few examples, have offered them fresh perspectives and even opened them up to activism. Moreover, some students in STEM have also been radicalized as a result of unionization movements on campus. That's why the US left must reject stereotyped characterization of these students, reach out to them, and welcome them into common struggles. It is a concrete method of building solidarity within the US.

CHINESE STUDENTS AND CAMPUS RADICALIZATION

There are enormous opportunities for such work on campuses across the US. Over the past decade, these institutions have become hotbeds of radicalization, with students joining struggles like Occupy, Climate Strikes, Black Lives Matter, the Bernie Sanders campaigns, and grad student unionization. In this context, those Chinese students dissatisfied with the dominant ideas either in China or the US can become a part of the student radicalization and join fellow activists in today's social and class struggles on and off campus. Some, for example, joined protests in solidarity with Hong Kong, seizing the chance to exercise their civil rights on a central question in China.

Another significant example is the way that many Chinese students were inspired to join feminist struggles in the US following the recent upsurge of feminist voices in China. In the beginning of March 2015, a group of young feminists in China were arrested and detained on the eve of International Women's Day. They had planned to put anti–sexual harassment stickers on public transportation. Given that the Communist Party officially supports women's liberation and equality, this repression shocked scholars and feminists globally and was widely covered in the Western media. The exposure of this crackdown was the product of an anonymous network of Chinese students, mainly in the US. They provided regular social media updates on the detainees. Since then, Chinese feminists in the US have gathered more supporters and advocated for gender equality in China through new media platforms. On January 21, 2017, dozens of Chinese feminists from all across North America joined the Women's March on Washington. In addition to supporting their global sisters in fighting Trump's presidency, these feminists hoped that their US-based advocacy would help organize and advance feminist causes in China.

Chinese students as university employees have also joined their coworkers in campus labor struggles, especially graduate student unionizing. The recent wave of organizing was kicked off by NYU's graduate union, UAW Local 2110, which became the first grad-student union recognized by a private university in the US. Because Chinese students are a central part of graduate programs in the US, they have been a key part of various organizing drives. They constitute more than one-third of all international graduate students and 16 percent of all students in STEM programs at the graduate level.[14] Chinese research assistants and teaching assistants have been a part of graduate-student unionization, and some of them have taken on leadership roles as organizers. In fact, Chinese students have been on the front lines of struggles from Harvard and Columbia to Indiana University.[15] Most recently, they have formed a key part of the University of California (UC) strikes in 2022.[16] Their participation in unionization efforts has given them confidence to take on political struggles, including organizing rallies against anti-Asian racism.

In response to increasing Chinese international student activism in general, and the rise of anti-Asian and anti-China rhetoric and behaviors in specific since the outbreak of COVID, a new organization, the Chinese Students and Activists (CSA) Network, was launched in 2020. Providing a space for Chinese international students and activists to learn about and engage with social movements and community organizing, CSA explicitly embraces a progressive agenda that challenges the "either Beijing or Washington" discourse. Its members believe that "much of the tensions between the US and China do not serve the people in both countries . . . to address economic, climate and health crises in the 21st century, [what we need] is a new path for Chinese international students, the Chinese immigrant community, the Asian American community, working class people of color, Indigenous communities and white progressives and liberals to build something new."[17] Since 2020, CSA has organized a series of webinars and fellowship/internship programs that connect to hundreds of undergraduate and graduate students, address their concerns and needs in participating in civil and political activities, and offer them a "toolkit" for future activism.[18]

The latest episode of Chinese student activism in the US has been their participation in demonstrations in support of the A4 protests back in China, which was led by urban young people in protest against the CCP's draconian COVID lockdowns. Joining these overseas demonstrations were not just veteran student activists but many ordinary students who had not previously participated in any activism. These students witnessed how Chinese domestic politics changed during the three years of the pandemic and, by joining protests, showed they were willing to risk their identity being disclosed and reported to the Chinese authorities. In the wake of the demonstrations, new networks, groups, and publications have sprung up. This is unprecedented and cuts against the prevailing view that Chinese students in the US are apolitical, self-interested, and cynical.

All the struggles laid out above are a source of tremendous hope and opportunity for international solidarity from below. A radical minority of Chinese students are beginning to develop critical consciousness through coursework and reading groups that unpack ideologies, defamiliarize nationalist myths, and cultivate a transnational perspective critical of oppression and exploitation. Such students can become new voices that can challenge dominant ideas in both countries. They are the core for building organizations, publishing articles, and fighting for change not only in the US but also in China.

Today, Chinese Americans and overseas Chinese students are battling on multiple fronts but, in particular, their activism confronts the pervasive and deeply rooted anti-Asian racism that has intensified amid the US-China rivalry in three ways. First, cultural exchanges between Chinese students studying in the US and the left can help humanize "China" and deepen our understanding of domestic struggles in China while pointing toward ways to support it. Recognizing the internal inequalities and diversities within China is a crucial way to avoid the twin pitfalls of the pro-US Chinese Right fueled by a Cold War ideology and the pro-China nationalism within the Chinese American communities, which ignores people's suffering in China. Second, as many Chinese students in STEM may have a chance to work in the US after graduation and even gain permanent residency, they could potentially contribute to labor struggles in Silicon Valley; this is why their organizing in graduate school is strategically important for the broader union movement. Third, overseas Chinese activism has been making direct connections to activists and organizers still in China. These efforts have been increasingly important to the movements inside China because as state censorship intensifies, virtual and physical spaces abroad can offer safe communities to foster plans and actions back home.

Chinese and Chinese Americans have played a key role in US social movements for many decades. Historically and today, the activists have faced the challenge of navigating identities and affiliations with China that have increasingly been regarded with suspicion by both sides of the interimperial rivalry. Nonetheless, as the few examples above illustrate, there is every reason to be hopeful about the radical and radicalizing potential of Chinese American activism in labor, feminist, anti-capitalist, and anti-imperialist movements. This is an important moment for the US left to build alliances with Chinese and Asian American activists, and vice versa, not just out of solidarity, but as a necessity in building a movement against the US-China conflict.

NEITHER WASHINGTON NOR BEIJING

International Solidarity against Imperialist Rivalry

C hina's rise within the US superintended international order has stoked intense interimperialist rivalry. This is shaping both powers' economics, geopolitics, and military planning and thereby international relations throughout the world. The US-China conflict is coinciding with enormous crises of capitalism that are calling into question the legitimacy of governments around the globe, opening a new period of turbulence within and between the two states. The rulers of both states have turned to nationalism to deflect popular anger onto oppressed people and their imperial rivals. At the same time, increased exploitation and oppression have and will produce intense struggles by workers and the oppressed in both the US and China. In this context the left must adopt a clear approach of building international solidarity from below against both imperial states and their ruling classes.

GLOBAL CAPITALISM'S MULTIPLE CRISES

The world economy is beset by multiple interconnected, mutually reinforcing, and cascading crises. The long neoliberal boom from the early 1980s through the 2000s ended with 2008's Great Recession, which ushered in a long economic depression characterized by weak recoveries and sharp contractions. This slump has exacerbated the domestic crises of social reproduction, with gutted welfare states incapable of providing adequate support to people ravaged by the economy. While the US is the paradigmatic case of this pattern in the West, China is not an exception as it has undergone neoliberalization with its own distinctive characteristics. As a result, workers throughout the world are forced to rely on themselves to survive, intensifying gender oppression, as women in particular bear the brunt of the burden of privatized social care. As a result, the fabric of societies is coming apart at the seams.

These conditions have driven the US and other states to impose a reactionary stability on various countries through the so-called War on Terror and so-called humanitarian intervention. These have only exacerbated conditions for the impacted countries and their peoples, as neoliberal austerity always accompanies storm troopers. Even worse, with Washington's unipolar world order undermined by its defeats in Iraq and Afghanistan, it now faces imperial rivals, most importantly China but also Russia, as well as regional powers jockeying for position against other states in their neighborhood, triggering war in Ukraine and increasing tensions over Taiwan. This race for capitalist supremacy has ensured that efforts to combat climate change are woefully inadequate. All states put profit and geopolitical power before people and the planet. The consequent global heating has generated massive storms, wildfires, and desertification, driving people from their homelands as climate refugees to add to the record numbers of migrants fleeing economic devastation and war. Instead of providing them sanctuary, the world's states have erected massive but porous border regimes, which block most people's freedom of movement and criminalize those that evade capture as cheap labor at the base of economies throughout the world.

The expansion of global capitalism into previously isolated ecosystems has enabled zoonotic spillover of viruses from animals to humans, creating conditions for pandemics, with COVID likely the first of many more to come. The COVID pandemic has exacerbated and deepened all of global capitalism's other problems, including economic and racial inequalities within and among countries. All these crises are ripping apart the neoliberal world order that the US has managed since the end of the Cold War. The institutions that the US has crafted to shore up that order—the IMF, the World Bank, the WTO, the WHO, and the UN—have lost legitimacy, have been paralyzed by interstate antagonisms, or have been sidelined by bilateral deals and alternative institutions put forward by China. As a result, the US has suffered relative decline and China has risen to become a regional and international rival with pretensions for challenging the US for global hegemony.

There is bipartisan consensus in Washington to resist China's relative increase in power, which has generated multiplying conflicts between the two states. While each country's rulers are attempting to ameliorate the intense inequalities in their societies with small reforms, they will be unable to deliver significant improvements in people's lives because of the competitive pressures of global capitalism. Therefore, pressure on living standards will continue to trigger dissent and outbursts of social and class struggle. Indeed, the decade after the Great Recession has witnessed one of the largest waves of revolt in recent history, from the Arab Spring through Occupy Wall Street and Black Lives Matter in the US, to widespread labor and ethnic unrest in Mainland China, powerfully demonstrated by the wave of protests against zero-COVID lockdowns and strikes against "closed-loop management."

AGAINST GREAT POWER NATIONALISMS

Faced with simmering and sometimes explosive discontent from below, the US and Chinese ruling classes have turned to great power nationalism to bind their workers and oppressed peoples to their capitalist and imperialist aims. Both parties of the US establishment have whipped up American patriotism against China. Beijing, too, has whipped up nationalism, with Xi Jinping reclaiming his state's status as a great power in Asia and throughout the world. The conflict between the two powers is, for now, muted by their deep economic interdependence, but their interests are increasingly becoming antagonistic. As a result, their rivalry will intensify, stoking economic, geopolitical, and potentially military conflicts throughout the world. Their competition for global supremacy will engulf all states and regions from Asia to the EU, Latin America, and Africa.

Confronted with this imperial clash and its dueling nationalisms, the international left must avoid two pitfalls. First, the US left, which is the principal audience for this book, must not line up behind Washington's imperial project. It is against the interests of US workers and oppressed people, and backing it violates the internationalist and anti-imperialist principles that are the bedrock of any genuine left. The US ruling class and its state exploit the country's working-class majority and have intensified racial, gender, and national oppression to splinter any resistance. The US state and corporations have also pushed for globalization of capital to take advantage of cheap labor, particularly in China, pitting the workers of the world against one another in a race to the bottom. The US state appointed itself the sheriff of this global capitalist order, enforcing its international and national inequalities by military means.

Now that very same state and ruling class hope to use nationalism buttressed by industrial policies and protectionism to win popular support for their conflict with China. Whatever their differences, both the Republicans and Democrats claim their pursuit of rivalry with China will serve the interests of US workers and oppressed peoples. In reality, such conflict will come at their expense. Any concessions to their nationalism will divide workers against one another internationally as well as domestically. Both parties offer corporations the chance to "come home" and exploit largely non-union, cheap US labor to compete against China. The US has encouraged "friend shoring" where supply chains are moved out of China and into low-cost but presumably more pro-US countries such as India, Mexico, or Vietnam. This will only make it easier for multinational corporations to reap profits from the divided workers of the world and make international unionization more difficult. Nationalism will only enhance racialized divisions between citizen and migrant labor. It has already caused a spike in anti-Chinese and anti-Asian racism. Such divisions will make it harder to organize the US's multiracial and multinational working class to build unions, raise wages and benefits, and win social reforms.

Even worse, such nationalism will wed US workers and oppressed peoples to US imperialism, its warmongering that threatens countries throughout the world, and its diversion of trillions of dollars that could go to worker's wages, benefits, and social programs, as well as climate reforms like the Green New Deal, into the Pentagon's war machine. And in the event of a war, politicians and bosses won't do the killing and dying. That will be left to workers and oppressed people. Thus, the US left should reject and oppose Washington's imperial project and the reactionary nationalism that justifies it.

The US and international left must avoid a second pitfall of supporting China as some kind of socialist alternative or anti-imperialist state. It is neither. As we've argued, China is certainly not socialist. Nor is China an oppressed nation standing up to US imperialism. The Chinese state collaborated with the US state and capitals in opening its economy to international investment and exploitation. Until recently, it backed the US on many international questions, including Washington's so-called War on Terror, which China used as cover to carry out its horrific attacks on Uyghurs and other Muslim populations. And now, China's clear aim is to challenge the US for imperial dominance over the capitalist world system.

It would be a disastrous mistake for the international left to align itself with China against the US. Such a position is great power nationalism in reverse, of supporting another capitalist state with imperialist ambitions. It will discredit the left in the eyes of people in China, the Global South, and the US. First of all, it would break solidarity with the struggles of Chinese workers, feminists, queer activists, Marxist students, and intellectuals—not to mention people in Hong Kong, Tibet, Xinjiang, and Taiwan. It would break solidarity with peoples oppressed by regimes China backs like those in Russia, Thailand, Myanmar, Cambodia, and Syria. It would break solidarity with workers, peasants, and indigenous people in the Global South dispossessed and exploited by China's BRI. Finally, it would alienate workers and oppressed peoples in the US already alarmed by China's capitalist police state. Adopting great power nationalism in reverse would make it easier for the US ruling class and its parties to discredit the left as anti-democratic apologists for an oppressive regime, charges that marginalized the Stalinist left throughout the twentieth century.

FOR INTERNATIONALIST ANTI-IMPERIALISM

Against both forms of great power nationalism, our aim is to advance internationalist anti-imperialism in response to the rivalry between Washington and Beijing. One potential approach would be to promote internationalism from above, a strategy of attempting to forge international cooperation between the two capitalist states. While everyone should welcome efforts to mitigate their conflict, state-centric internationalism from above is unlikely to succeed in averting disaster for several reasons. At the most basic level, these two states and economies have increasingly antagonistic interests. While the US and its corporations have heretofore dominated the world and have done so in collaboration with China, they now find themselves in growing conflict with one another. Washington's hegemony and at least some of its corporate dominance, especially in high tech, are being threatened. That's why there is a new Washington consensus against China.

The same goes for China. It wants to challenge US hegemony in order to reclaim its status as a great power and move up the value chain in the world economy. This growing rivalry shapes both states' economic, geopolitical, and military strategies. Therefore, neither of Washington's two imperialist parties nor China's regime will be able to cooperate in addressing the world's most pressing social and ecological crises. Of course, we should support any agreement that decreases the conflict—particularly its militaristic aspects—but we should be under no illusions that these will amount to anything more than tactical maneuvers in a strategic rivalry. The competitive pressures of global capitalism, which are the underlying causes of the two states' rivalry, guarantee that any pacts or compromises will be temporary cooling off periods in the conflict before it heats up again.

In the US, a danger for the left is that such vain hopes for interstate cooperation will lead people into the Democratic Party in the false expectation that it will curtail militarism and pursue cooperation across borders. As Joe Biden's record has demonstrated, the Democrats are equally, if not more, committed to great power rivalry with China than the Republicans, which have an isolationist wing that wants to disengage from such conflicts altogether. The Biden administration has aggressively whipped up conflict with both China and Russia, making a military conflagration more likely, most obviously in Eastern Europe and the Asia Pacific. While we must make demands on the US state and its capitalist parties for reform and against their militarism, placing our hopes in either of them to curb the imperial antagonism will only lead to co-optation and disappointment.

The second and more effective way to oppose interimperial rivalry is internationalism from below. Its starting point is building solidarity across borders between workers and oppressed peoples and nations against all great powers. For the US left, as the German socialist Karl Liebknecht famously said, the main enemy is at home—the US state, its ruling class, its corporations, and its capitalist parties. The US left can make a critical contribution to our own liberation and those of people in other countries by preventing Washington from enforcing the current order of global capitalism, especially via its militarism. The US state and ruling class remain our main oppressors and exploiters, not any other state or ruling class. The same priority holds for workers and oppressed peoples in China; their main enemy is their own ruling class and its state. At the same time, the left must not allow the borders of the nation state to confine our political imagination: our organizing must be as international as global capitalism itself. Our task is to build solidarity from below, uniting US and Chinese people together in a common struggle against both states and global capitalism. This project is the only way out of the antagonism and only way to overcome the competitive dynamic of global capitalism that is driving it.

While clearly beset with various political obstacles, the material and social conditions are in place to build such solidarity. Objectively, workers in both countries are bound together by the system's international structures of production and logistics of transport, distribution, and sale. Take Apple as just one example. It does R&D in the US; subcontracts production to a Taiwanese conglomerate that runs giant factories, mainly in China; transports its products through international air and shipping conglomerates to its own warehouses for distribution; and conducts sales through its own stores and website or those of other corporations, like telecom giant Verizon, as well as Amazon. The relationship, of course, is not just one way. Chinese capital is heavily invested in the US, mainly in acquiring US-based companies, as well as real estate. And the US is the largest market for Chinese exports. Based on this deep economic integration, the two societies are also increasingly interlinked. Numbering roughly 2.5 million, people from China make up the third-largest immigrant group in the US and by far the largest group of foreign students.

Global capitalism's crises are provoking waves of struggle from below that are opening up subjective possibilities for organizing international solidarity. In the US, the capitalist establishment is going through one of the sharpest legitimacy crises in its history and has faced a decade of struggle against class and social inequality from Occupy to teachers strikes and Black Lives Matter and, since the pandemic, an increase in workplace organizing, contract rejections, and walkouts.[1] Similarly in China, staggering economic inequality amid slowing growth and spiking youth unemployment have generated major discontent and struggles against the bureaucratic-capitalist elite, a sentiment the state has aimed to co-opt and tame with its unfulfilled rhetoric of "Common Prosperity." These have taken various forms from the "lying flat" resistance of young people balking at joining cutthroat competition for education and careers to the workers rebellions amid the lockdowns, the A4 uprising, and elderly people's resistance to cuts in social welfare in the wake of the state's abandonment of zero-COVID. Such struggles, often over similar grievances and in labor battles often against the same corporations, make it possible to turn shared objective interests into actual solidarity from below. Whether these possibilities are capitalized upon is a political and organizational question—a question that can only be answered by conscious activism and struggle.

ORGANIZING SOLIDARITY WITHIN AND ACROSS BORDERS

To seize these opportunities requires an international left embedded in the struggles in both of these countries as well as the rest of the world. Some of this organizing can be pursued immediately, while other efforts will remain anticipatory forms of solidarity that can lay the foundation for concrete action in the future. In the US the left has enormous responsibilities and possibilities. First and foremost, the left must oppose the US state and its imperialist policies. Organizing to redirect resources away from policing and war and toward social protection and decarbonization is good for people in the US *and* around the world. In particular, the left must combat racism and xenophobia to unite the US's multiracial and multinational working class, of which Chinese and Asian American workers are an important part.

The most immediate way to do that is organizing in the large Chinese and Chinese American population, including nearly three hundred thousand Chinese international students. A left embedded in these communities has and will play an essential role in combating the Sinophobia Washington has whipped up. It can oppose the witch hunt against Chinese tech workers, professors, and students in the US as well as help build actions like the protests led by Chinese students in support of China's A4 protests. It can help organize labor struggles, especially on campuses where Chinese students have played a leading role, most recently in the university strikes that swept California. Such campaigns among graduate students are particularly important not only in building solidarity within the US, but also internationally, as many Chinese activists are involved in labor organizing in China and can use their experiences in the US to build resistance and solidarity there.

That work can then feed back into the US by breaking down divisions among the countries' labor movements. *Labor Notes* pioneered this work of establishing connections with Chinese labor activists and NGOs before they were repressed. It put Chinese labor activists on speaking tours across the US, giving presentations at meetings held by unions, labor solidarity formations, and student/labor coalitions. It culminated with presentations at *Labor Notes*'s bi-annual conferences. With the suppression of the labor NGOs and crackdown on labor militancy and imprisonment of activists in China, such tours are now much more difficult to organize, but the *Labor Notes* tours set a precedent to be built on in the future. They demonstrated the reality of common interests, established connections among militants in both countries, and showed the possibility of joint struggle.

We have seen flashes of such cross-border solidarity in recent years. For example, in 2019, Chinese tech workers put together a project on GitHub, a global software service and code collaboration platform, protesting Chinese tech companies' 996 policy that required them to work from 9:00 a.m. to 9:00 p.m., six days a week. Over 230,000 mainly Chinese workers started the project, triggering Alibaba and Tencent to block the site on their browsers. Worried that Microsoft might do the same, Microsoft workers penned a letter on GitHub in Chinese and English opposing any censorship and supporting the struggle of their Chinese counterparts. Over 80,000 workers from all over the world signed the letter. Workers from Britain, Turkey, Singapore, France, and Spain translated the letter into their languages and uploaded it to the GitHub page.[2] Thus, even in the high-tech economy that is the site of such interimperial conflict, workers demonstrated the possibility of joint action against their exploiters in both countries.

The US left must not only build bridges of solidarity with exploited workers but also the movements of oppressed groups, nations, and peoples. Out of the deep crisis of social reproduction, a new women's movement is beginning to be born in both the US and in China. Establishing linkages between these struggles must be a central priority for the US left and feminist organizations. So should solidarity with the struggles of nations and people oppressed by the Chinese state, like Hong Kong, Taiwan, Tibet, and Xinjiang. Many activists from these groups have fled into exile in the US and other countries. These large diasporic communities internationalize their homelands' struggles, organizing campaigns and demonstrations in solidarity with their people. Of course, these are politically heterogenous with a range of political forces from the left to the right. But all mass movements are politically heterogeneous and given that their basic demands are progressive and democratic, a left organized in them can increase the influence of progressive and socialist ideas.

If the left does not do so, the US state and the right will fill the vacuum. For example, they have already pretended to be in solidarity with the struggles of Hong Kongers and Uyghurs. Of course, this is pure hypocrisy as Washington's long track record of supporting British imperialism in Hong Kong and its Islamophobic War on Terror prove. In fact, despite its avowed support for Hong Kong during the height of the protests in 2019, Congress has failed to create a program to grant visas or citizenship to Hong Kongers facing state repression. But, absent other options, people will turn to Washington out of desperation. That's precisely why the US left must collaborate with the diasporic left in these communities to provide an internationalist alternative to the US state and the right.

TOWARD AN INTERNATIONAL LEFT

As part of developing a current of internationalism from below, the US left should pursue collaboration with the left in China and in the Asia Pacific as a whole. Language differences and political repression make it difficult to engage with many groups in China, but there is a robust network of leftist groups and publications that bridge this division. These include the Hong Kong diaspora group and website *Lausan*, the Taiwanese publication *New Bloom*, and the US-based Chinese Students and Activists Network (CSA). Other international publications providing critical analysis of China in English include *Gongchao*, *Chuang*, and *Made in China Journal*.[3]

A crucial way to deepen ties on the left internationally is organizing discussions, meetings, teach-ins, and conferences about the conflict between the US and China and the urgency of organizing international solidarity against it. The conference that first brought some of the co-authors together led to the publication of a valuable anthology of left perspectives from *Verso Books* entitled *The China Question* in 2022. The Critical China Scholars have sponsored important educational webinars and panels. Similar meetings can and must be organized in the Asia Pacific, Latin America, Africa, the Middle East, and Europe. Moreover, the left internationally must include discussions of the interimperialist rivalry and its politics in its conferences, especially international ones. In that way, we can develop a current throughout the world of internationalist anti-imperialism.

Those are some of the tasks of the US and international left. For activists in China, the conditions are far more challenging. They face extreme levels of state repression today, especially when it comes to solidarity with international movements and especially the internationalist left. The state has made it practically impossible for international organizations or even informal activist networks to operate above ground in China. On top of that, it frequently charges labor, feminist, and leftwing activists with being pawns of "hostile foreign forces," committed to fomenting a "color revolution." Even while overseas, Chinese activists have been subjected to surveillance and harassment by agents of the state. So, while the CCP has embraced the transnational circulation of capital and commodities, it is fundamentally hostile to social and labor movements crossing borders. As a result, the US and international left cannot realistically expect solidarity in its ideal form of frequent and substantive acts of political reciprocity founded on mutually shared interests. If, for instance, workers at a Tesla plant in Shanghai go on strike in support of their counterparts in the US or Germany, they would be subjected to incredibly harsh repression. We cannot expect them at this point to take such inordinate risks.

Much of the US and international left still possess democratic rights to dissent and organize, however much such rights are under threat. We must take advantage of this space to advance solidarity in an anticipatory manner—acting now to support those exploited and oppressed by China with the expectation that activists there will find ways to reciprocate in the coming years. Our job is to stitch together the networks of activists, however rudimentary, in the US, China, and elsewhere who can in the future make reciprocal solidarity from below a force to oppose global capitalism, great power nationalism, and the interimperial rivalries they stoke.

We must proclaim loudly and repeatedly that the fate of marginalized and exploited people around the world are in fact linked. Nowhere is this fact more clearly demonstrated than in the case of China and the US. However committed to their rivalry, they both learn from and imitate each other's strategies and tactics. When the Chinese government launched its "People's War on Terror" in Xinjiang, it learned from Washington's Abu Ghraib, Guantánamo, and the whole Islamophobic War on Terror. When the US votes an avowed sexual predator into the White House and crackdown on abortion rights, the all-male standing committee of the Politburo felt emboldened to rollback women's rights in China. Their system binds workers and the oppressed in both countries to each other. The exploitation of electronics workers in Shenzhen or Suzhou undergirds the concentration of capital that fuels tech-fueled gentrification and displacement in Oakland or Seattle. And we face increasingly similar conditions in both places. The poor and socially vulnerable populations of Zhengzhou and New Orleans face the rising flood waters of catastrophic climate change, while the rich continue their lavish lifestyles safely barricaded in high rises or bucolic second homes. So now more than ever before, it is time to build the political and organizational groundwork for solidarity against the imperialist scramble for dominance over a global capitalism that threatens the well-being of the entire world.

SUGGESTED READINGS
AND RESOURCES

Chapter 1: China Is Capitalist
Ho-fung Hung, *The China Boom: Why China Will Not Rule the World* (New York: Columbia University Press, 2015).
Ralf Rukus, *The Communist Road to Capitalism* (Oakland: PM Press, 2021).
Sorghum and Steel: The Socialist Developmental Regime and the Forging of China, Chuang, https://chuangcn.org/journal/one/sorghum-and-steel/.

Chapter 2: The Emergence of a New Great Power
Ho-fung Hung, *Clash of Empires: From "Chimerica" to the "New Cold War"* (Cambridge: Cambridge University Press, 2022).
Au Loong Yu, *China's Rise: Strength and Fragility* (London: Merlin Press, 2013).
Charlie Hore, *The Road to Tiananmen Square* (London: Bookmarks, 1991).

Chapter 3: Class Struggle in the Countryside, Cities, and Workplaces
Dead Generations, Chuang, Issue 1, https://chuangcn.org/journal/one/.
Ivan Franceschini and Christian Sorace, *Proletarian China: A Century of Chinese Labour* (London: Verso Books, 2022).
Joel Andreas, *Disenfranchised: The Rise and Fall of Industrial Citizenship in China* (Oxford: Oxford University Press, 2019).
Zhongjin Li, Eli Friedman, and Hao Ren, *China on Strike: Narratives of Workers' Resistance* (Chicago: Haymarket Books, 2016).

Chapter 4: Feminist Resistance and the Crisis of Social Reproduction
Zheng Wang. *Finding Women in the State: A Socialist Feminist Revolution in the People's Republic of China, 1949–1964* (Berkeley: University of California Press, 2016).
Angela Xiao Wu, and Yige Dong, "What Is Made-in-China Feminism (s)? Gender Discontent and Class Friction in Post-socialist China," *Critical Asian Studies* 51, no. 4 (2019): 471–92.
Ngai Pun, *Made in China: Women Factory Workers in a Global Workplace* (Durham: Duke University Press, 2005).

Yige Dong. "The Dilemma of Foxconn Moms: Social Reproduction and the Rise of 'Gig Manufacturing' in China," *Critical Sociology* 49, no. 7/8 (2023): 1231–49, https://doi.org/10.1177/08969205221140927

Chapter 5: China's National Questions

Emily T. Yeh, *Taming Tibet* (Ithaca: Cornell University Press, 2013).

Darren Byler, Ivan Franceschini, and Nicholas Loubere, *Xinjiang Year Zero* (Canberra: ANU Press, 2022). Free download: https://press.anu.edu.au/publications/xinjiang-year-zero.

Ilham Tohti, *We Uyghurs Have No Say: An Imprisoned Writer Speaks* (London: Verso Books, 2022).

Wen Liu, J. N. Chien, Christina Chung, and Ellie Tse, eds, *Reorienting Hong Kong's Resistance: Leftism, Decoloniality, and Internationalism* (Singapore: Springer Singapore, 2022).

Ching Kwan Lee, *Hong Kong: Global China's Restive Frontier* (Cambridge: Cambridge *Elements*, 2022).

Ho-fung Hung, *City on the Edge: Hong Kong under Chinese Rule* (Cambridge: Cambridge University Press, 2022).

Ming-sho Ho, *Challenging Beijing's Mandate of Heaven: Taiwan's Sunflower Movement and Hong Kong's Umbrella Movement* (Philadelphia: Temple University Press, 2019).

Chapter 6: The US v. China

Ho-fung Hung, *Clash of Empires: From "Chimerica" to the "New Cold War"* (Cambridge: Cambridge University Press, 2022).

Au Loong Yu, *China's Rise: Strength and Fragility* (London: Merlin Press, 2013).

Chapter 7: China and Global Capitalism's Ecological and Climate Crises

Richard Smith, *China's Engine of Environmental Collapse* (London: Pluto Press, 2020).

Olivier Krischer and Luigi Tomba, eds., *Shades of Green: Notes on China's Eco-civilisation*, *Made in China Journal* (2021), https://madeinchinajournal.com/wp-content/uploads/2021/01/SHADES_OF_GREEN_2020.pdf.

Chapter 8: Pandemics in an Epoch of Imperial Rivalry

Chuang, *Social Contagion* (Chicago: Charles H. Kerr, 2021).

Rob Wallace, *Big Farms Make Big Flu* (New York: Monthly Review Press, 2016).

Rob Wallace, *Dead Epidemiologists* (New York: Monthly Review Press, 2020).

Li Zhang, *The Origins of COVID-19: China and Global Capitalism* (Palo Alto, CA: Stanford University Press, 2021).

Chapter 9: "China" in the US

Gordon C. Chang, *Ghosts of Gold Mountain: The Epic Story of the Chinese Who Built the Transcontinental Railroad* (Boston: Mariner Books, 2019).

Karen L. Ishizuka, *Serve the People: Making Asian America in the Long Sixties* (New Left Books, 2018).
Diane C. Fujino and Robyn Magalit Rodriguez, eds., *Contemporary Asian American Activism: Building Movements for Liberation* (Seattle: University of Washington Press, 2022).
Yingyi Ma, *Ambitious and Anxious: How Chinese College Students Succeed and Struggle in American Higher Education* (Columbia University Press, 2020).

Conclusion: Neither Washington Nor Beijing

Below, find a selection of websites for organizations and publications that provide regularly updated information. These sources are politically diverse, but all provide left perspectives, broadly conceived.

Mainland China:

Made in China: https://madeinchinajournal.com/.
China Labour Bulletin: https://clb.org.hk/.
Chuang: https://chuangcn.org/.
Gongchao: https://www.gongchao.org/.

Hong Kong:

Lausan: https://lausancollective.com/.
New Left Society: https://newleftsoccuhk.blogspot.com/.

Taiwan:

New Bloom: https://newbloommag.net/.
Taiwan Labor Front: https://labor.ngo.tw/about-labour-en/introduction-en.
Taiwan International Workers' Association: https://tiwa.org.tw/ (Chinese).

International:

Critical China Scholars: https://criticalchinascholars.org/.
Asian Labour Review: https://labourreview.org/.
Chinese Students and Activists (CSA) Network: https://www.csanetwork.org/.

NOTES

Introduction

1 See https://rageagainstwar.com/#Speakers.
2 Eli Friedman, Kevin Lin, and Ashley Smith, eds., *The China Question: Toward Left Perspectives* (New York: Verso Books, 2022).

Chapter 1: China Is Capitalist

1 Ralf Ruckus, *The Communist Road to Capitalism: How Social Unrest and Containment Have Pushed China's (R)evolution since 1949* (Oakland: PM Press, 2021).
2 Sara Hsu, "High Income Inequality Still Festering in China," *Forbes*, November 18, 2016, https://www.forbes.com/sites/sarahsu/2016/11/18/high-income-inequality-still-festering-in-china/?sh=7874396f1e50.
3 Bryce Baschuk, "China Loses Landmark WTO Dispute against EU," Bloomberg, June 16, 2020, https://www.bloomberg.com/news/articles/2020-06-16/not-with-a-bang-china-loses-landmark-wto-dispute-against-eu.
4 "Full Text: Xi Jinping's Keynote Speech at the World Economic Forum," http://www.china.org.cn/node_7247529/content_40569136.htm.
5 "Xi Stresses Decisive Role of Market in Resource Allocation," *Xinhua*, May 23, 2020, http://www.xinhuanet.com/english/2020-05/23/c_139082029.htm.
6 Ho-fung Hung, *The China Boom: Why China Will Not Rule the World* (New York: Columbia University Press, 2015).
7 "Leading Chinese Real Estate Companies on the Fortune China 500 Ranking as of 2023, by Revenue," Statista, https://www.statista.com/statistics/454494/china-fortune-500-leading-chinese-real-estate-companies/.
8 Sarosh Kuruvilla, Ching Kwan Lee, and Mary E. Gallagher, eds, *From Iron Rice Bowl to Informalization: Markets, Workers, and the State in a Changing China* (Ithaca: Cornell University Press, 2011).
9 "2016 nian nongmingong jiance diaocha baogao," National Bureau of Statistics, April 28, 2017, http://www.stats.gov.cn/tjsj/zxfb/201704/t20170428_1489334.html.
10 Eli Friedman, "The Urbanization of People," in Eli Friedman, *The Urbanization of People* (New York: Columbia University Press, 2022).

11 "Society at a Glance 2016: OECD Social Indicators," OECD, https://
    www.oecd-ilibrary.org/social-issues-migration-health/society-at-a-
    glance-2016/social-spending_soc_glance-2016-19-en;jsessionid=QqkhJFhz
    8uQXmBMcrVGcgrTphzVm1v_SN-5grhsQ.ip-10-240-5-19.

12 "Left to Rot: The Crisis in China's Pension System," *Chuang*, March 2,
    2020, https://chuangcn.org/2020/03/left-to-rot/.

13 Dorothy Solinger, *Poverty and Pacification: The Chinese State Abandons the
    Old Working Class* (London: Rowman & Littlefield, 2022).

14 Xiao Guiqing, "fangzhi luoru 'fulizhuyi' yang lanhan xianjing," *Beijing
    Ribao*, November 16, 2021. http://theory.people.com.cn/n1/2021/1116/
    c40531-32283350.html.

15 Zhongjin Li, Eli Friedman, and Hao Ren, *China on Strike: Narratives of
    Workers' Resistance* (Chicago: Haymarket Books, 2016).

16 "Zengcheng Riot: China Forces Quell Migrant Unrest," BBC, June 14,
    2011, https://www.bbc.com/news/world-asia-pacific-13763147.

17 Karl Hu, "China: Leader of Delivery Riders Alliance Detained, Solidarity
    Movement Repressed," *Labor Notes*, April 15, 2021, https://www.
    labornotes.org/2021/04/china-leader-delivery-riders-alliance-detained-
    solidarity-movement-repressed.

18 Yingjie Guo, "Farewell to Class, Except the Middle Class: The Politics of
    Class Analysis in Contemporary China," *Asia-Pacific Journal* 26, no. 2
    (2009): 1–19.

19 Xiaoli Zhao, "On the Composition of the Deputies in the National
    People's Congress of China," *Tsinghua China Law Review* (2012).

20 Sui-Lee Wee, "China's Parliament Is a Growing Billionaires' Club," *New
    York Times*, March 1, 2018, https://www.nytimes.com/2018/03/01/
    business/china-parliament-billionaires.html.

21 David Barboza, "Billions in Hidden Riches for the Family of Chinese
    Leader," *New York Times*, October 25, 2012, https://www.nytimes.
    com/2012/10/26/business/global/family-of-wen-jiabao-holds-a-hidden-
    fortune-in-china.html.

22 Friedrich Engels, *Anti-Dühring* (New York: International Publishers,
    1976), 303.

23 Ming-sho Ho, "Manufacturing Loyalty: The Political Mobilization of
    Labor in Taiwan, 1950—1986," *Modern China* 36, no. 6 (2010): 559–88.

24 Ha-Joon Chang, *Kicking Away the Ladder* (New York: Anthem Press,
    2002).

25 Dorothy J. Solinger, "Labour Market Reform and the Plight of the Laid-
    Off Proletariat," *China Quarterly* 170 (2002): 304–26.

26 Ching Kwan Lee, *Against the Law: Labor Protests in China's Rustbelt and
    Sunbelt* (Berkeley: University of California Press, 2007).

27 Mary E. Gallagher, "Time Is Money, Efficiency Is Life": The
    Transformation of Labor Relations in China," *Studies in Comparative
    International Development* 39 (2004): 11–44.

28 Joel Andreas, *Disenfranchised: The Rise and Fall of Industrial Citizenship in China* (Oxford: Oxford University Press, 2019).

29 "82 Chinese SOEs Listed among 2021 Fortune Global 500," State-owned Assets Supervision and Administration Commission of the State Council, August 3, 2021. http://en.sasac.gov.cn/2021/08/03/c_7528.htm.

30 "Chinese Companies Listed on Major U.S. Stock Exchanges," U.S.-China Economic and Security Review Commission, May 5, 2021. https://www.uscc.gov/sites/default/files/2021-05/Chinese_Companies_on_US_Stock_Exchanges_5-2021.pdf.

31 "China Trade & Investment Summary," Office of the United States Trade Representative. https://ustr.gov/countries-regions/china-mongolia-taiwan/peoples-republic-china

32 Yue Quan and Ziyu Zhang, "China Encourages Foreign Investment in Real Estate through Private Equity Funds," *Caixin*, February 21, 2023, https://www.caixinglobal.com/2023-02-21/china-encourages-foreign-investment-in-real-estate-through-private-equity-funds-102000460.html.

33 "The Capitalist Transformation of Rural China: Evidence from 'Agrarian Change in Contemporary China,'" *Chuang*, August 8, 2015, https://chuangcn.org/2015/08/jac-review/.

Chapter 2: The Emergence of a New Great Power

1 Ralf Ruckus, *The Communist Road to Capitalism* (Oakland: PM Press, 2021), 2.

2 Charlie Hore, *The Road to Tiananmen Square* (London: Bookmarks, 1991), 44.

3 Ho-fung Hung, *The China Boom: Why China Will Not Rule the World* (New York: Columbia University Press, 2016), 42.

4 Robert L. Worden, Andrea Matles Savada, and Ronald E. Dolan, eds., *China: A Country Study* (Washington: GPO for the Library of Congress, 1987), https://countrystudies.us/china/25.htm.

5 Kimberley Ens Manning and Felix Wemheuer, eds., *Eating Bitterness: New Perspectives on China's Great Leap Forward and Famine* (Chicago: University of Chicago Press, 2011).

6 Nigel Harris, *The Mandate of Heaven: Marx and Mao in Modern China* (Chicago: Haymarket Books, 2015), 55–68.

7 Ruckus, 60–71.

8 Liang Zhang, Andrew Nathan, Perry Link, Orville Schell, *The Tiananmen Papers* (New York: Public Affairs, 2002).

9 Gideon Rachman, *Easternization: War and Peace in the Asian Century* (London: Penguin Random House, 2016), 30.

10 Joe McDonald, "Jiang Zemin, Who Guided China's Economic Rise, Dies," Associated Press, November 30th, 2022, https://apnews.com/article/china-beijing-hong-kong-obituaries-jiang-zemin-4ee4c5dcaf567e02efa3c5c7186af30a.

11   Chunlung Zhang, "How Much Do State-Owned Enterprises Contribute to China's GDP and Employment," World Bank, July 15, 2019, https://documents.worldbank.org/en/publication/documents-reports/documentdetail/449701565248091726/how-much-do-state-owned-enterprises-contribute-to-china-s-gdp-and-employment.

12   Amir Guluzade, "The Role of China's State-Owned Companies Explained," World Economic Forum, May 7, 2019, https://www.weforum.org/agenda/2019/05/why-chinas-state-owned-companies-still-have-a-key-role-to-play/.

13   Li Yuan, "Jack Ma, China's Richest Man, Belongs to the Communist Party. Of Course.," New York Times, November 27, 2018, https://www.nytimes.com/2018/11/27/business/jack-ma-communist-party-alibaba.html.

14   Scott Kennedy, "The US and China: Not Number One," Center for Strategic and International Studies, December 21, 2020, https://www.csis.org/blogs/trustee-china-hand/us-and-china-not-number-one.

15   Richard J. Chang, "The Countries with the Most Billionaires 2022," Forbes, April 5, 2022, https://www.forbes.com/sites/richardjchang/2022/04/05/the-countries-with-the-most-billionaires-2022/?sh=55510759b57e.

16   Alan Taylor, "Rising Protests in China," The Atlantic, February 17, 2012, https://www.theatlantic.com/photo/2012/02/rising-protests-in-china/100247/.

17   David Barboza, "China Unveils $586 Billion Stimulus Plan," New York Times, November 10, 2008, https://www.nytimes.com/2008/11/10/world/asia/10iht-10china.17673270.html.

18   Christine Wong, "The Fiscal Stimulus Programme and Public Governance Issues in China," OECD Journal on Budgeting, vol. 11/3 (2011), https://read.oecd-ilibrary.org/governance/the-fiscal-stimulus-programme-and-public-governance-issues-in-china_budget-11-5kg3nhljqrjl#page1.

19   Harold Trikunas, "Testing the Limits of China and Brazil's Partnership," Brookings, July 20, 2020, https://www.brookings.edu/articles/testing-the-limits-of-china-and-brazils-partnership/.

20   Ana Garcia, Miguel Borba, Patrick Bond, "Western Imperialism and the Role of Subimperialism in the Global South," New Politics 18, no. 70 (Winter 2021), https://newpol.org/issue_post/western-imperialism-and-the-role-of-sub-imperialism-in-the-global-south/.

21   Lee Wengraf, Extracting Profit: Imperialism Neoliberalism, and the New Scramble for Africa (Chicago: Haymarket Books, 2018), 93–165.

22   Megan Cerullo, "China Now Has the Most Companies on the Fortune 500 List," CBS News, August 3, 2022, https://www.cbsnews.com/news/walmart-tops-fortune-500-list-of-biggest-companies-for-ninth-consecutive-year/.

23   Elizabeth Economy, The Third Revolution: Xi Jinping and the New Chinese State (New York: Oxford University Press, 2018), 188.

24   Elizabeth Economy, *The Third Revolution: Xi Jinping and the New Chinese State*.

25   Economy, 190–98.

26   "China's Growing Global Influence: What's at Stake?," US Global Leadership Coalition, https://www.usglc.org/chinas-growing-influence-is-america-getting-left-behind/.

27   Yu Jie and John Wallace, "What Is China's Belt and Road Initiative (BRI)?," Chatham House, September 13, 2021, https://www.chathamhouse.org/2021/09/what-chinas-belt-and-road-initiative-bri.

28   Ho-fung Hung, *Clash of Empires: From "Chimerica" to the "New Cold War"* (Cambridge: Cambridge University Press, 2022), 47–56.

29   Terry Mobley, "The Belt and Road Initiative: Insights from China's Backyard," *Strategic Studies Quarterly* 13, no. 3 (Fall 2019): 52–72.

30   Jonathan Hillman, *The Emperor's New Road: China and the Project of the Century* (New Haven: Yale University Press, 2020).

31   Lingling Wei, "China Reins in Its Belt and Road Program, $1 Trillion Later," *Wall Street Journal*, September 26, 2022, https://www.wsj.com/articles/china-belt-road-debt-11663961638.

32   Scott Kennedy, "Made in China 2025," Center for Strategic and International Studies, June 1, 2015, https://www.csis.org/analysis/made-china-2025.

33   Chris Miller, *Chip War: The Fight for the World's Most Critical Technology* (New York: Scribner, 2022), 277–81.

34   Miller, 311–17.

35   Paul Mozur and John Liu, "The Chip Titan Whose Life's Work is at the Center of a Tech Cold War," *New York Times*, August 4, 2023, https://www.nytimes.com/2023/08/04/technology/the-chip-titan-whose-lifes-work-is-at-the-center-of-a-tech-cold-war.html?smid=fb-share&fbclid=IwAR0cVMG8Y7IFJayHAfvVKYzTwOz3-jT1fWxkQGE-EZIoK7rgpx-rpZ5wAX0.

36   Miller, 302.

37   "China Party Says Nearly 5 Million Probed for Graft," Associated Press, October 17, 2022, https://apnews.com/article/health-china-business-Covid-economy-6618e65ef6148e0c75fce4dc2a280 11f

38   Scott Livingston, "The New Challenge of Communist Corporate Governance," Center for Strategic and International Studies, January 15, 2021, https://www.csis.org/analysis/new-challenge-communist-corporate-governance.

39   Darren Byler, *Terror Capitalism: Uyghur Dispossession and Masculinity in a Chinese City* (Durham: Duke University Press, 2022).

40   Jun Nie and Andrew Palmer, "Consumer Spending in China: The Past and Future," Federal Reserve Bank of Kansas City, 28, https://www.kansascityfed.org/documents/551/2016-Consumer%20Spending%20in%20China:%20The%20Past%20and%20the%20Future.pdf.

41 "China Stimulus Brings Limited Help to Lockdown-Hit Consumers," Bloomberg News, May 24, 2022, https://www.bloomberg.com/news/articles/2022-05-24/china-s-stimulus-brings-limited-relief-to-lockdown-hit-consumers.

42 Jessie Yeung, "China Approved Equivalent of Two New Coal Plants a Week in 2022, Report Finds," CNN, February 27, 2023, https://www.cnn.com/2023/02/27/energy/china-new-coal-plants-climate-report-intl-hnk/index.html.

43 *Regional Comprehensive Economic Partnership (RCEP)*, Congressional Research Service, October 17, 2022, https://crsreports.congress.gov/product/pdf/IF/IF11891.

44 Ashley Smith, "After Russia's Invasion of Ukraine," Against the Current, no. 219 (July/August 2022), https://againstthecurrent.org/atc219/after-russias-invasion-of-ukraine/.

45 Diego Lopes da Silva, Nan Tian, Lucie Béraud-Sudreau, Alexandra Marksteiner, and Siao Liang, *Trends in World Military Expenditure, 2021*, SIPRI, April 2022, https://www.sipri.org/sites/default/files/2022-04/fs_2204_milex_2021_0.pdf.

46 Pieter D. Wezeman, Alexandra Kuimova, and Siemon T. Wezeman, *Trends in International Arms Transfers, 2021*, SIPRI, March 2022, https://www.sipri.org/sites/default/files/2022-03/fs_2203_at_2021.pdf.

47 Ho-fung Hung, *The China Boom: Why China Will Not Rule the World* (New York: Columbia University Press, 2015), 141.

48 Associated Press, "US Admiral Says China Has Fully Militarized Islands," *Politico*, March 20, 2022, https://www.politico.com/news/2022/03/20/china-islands-militarized-missiles-00018737.

49 David Vine, *Base Nation: How US Military Bases Abroad Harm America and the World* (New York: Metropolitan Books, 2015).

Chapter 3: Class Struggle in the Countryside, Cities, and Workplaces

1 "China's Push for Stability Undermines Law, Sociologist Says," Bloomberg News, November 29, 2012, https://www.bloomberg.com/news/articles/2012-11-29/china-s-push-for-stability-undermines-law-sociologist-says-1-.

2 Meg E. Rithmire, *Land Bargains and Chinese Capitalism: The Politics of Property Rights under Reform* (Cambridge: Cambridge University Press, 2015).

3 "Landesa 6th 17-Province China Survey," https://www.landesa.org/press-and-media/6th-china-survey/.

4 Nao, "Land Grabs in Contemporary China," Libcom.org, January 6, 2015, https://libcom.org/article/land-grabs-contemporary-china.

5 "Revisiting the Wukan Uprising of 2011: An Interview with Zhuang Liehong," *Chuang*, Issue 1, https://chuangcn.org/journal/one/revisiting-the-wukan-uprising-of-2011/.

6   Statista, "Degree of urbanization in China in selected years from 1980 to 2023." https://www.statista.com/statistics/270162/urbanization-in-china/.

7   Chunlin Zhang, "How Much Do State-Owned Enterprises Contribute to China's GDP and Employment," World Bank, July 15, 2019, https://documents.worldbank.org/en/publication/documents-reports/documentdetail/449701565248091726/how-much-do-state-owned-enterprises-contribute-to-china-s-gdp-and-employment.

8   Yueran Zhang, "Leninists in a Chinese Factory: Reflections on the Jasic Labour Organising Strategy," *Made in China Journal*, June 25, 2020, https://madeinchinajournal.com/2020/06/25/leninists-in-a-chinese-factory/.

Chapter 4: Feminist Resistance and the Crisis of Social Reproduction

1   "Society at a Glance 2016: OECD Social Indicators," OECD iLibrary, 109, https://www.oecd-ilibrary.org/social-issues-migration-health/society-at-a-glance-2016/social-spending_soc_glance-2016-19-en;jsessionid=Qqkh JFhz8uQXmBMcrVGcgrTphzVm1v_SN-5grhsQ.ip-10-240-5-19.

2   Ruo Mei, "China's 35M Domestic Workers, Silent No More," Six Tone, July 22, 2020, https://www.sixthtone.com/news/1005964.

3   "Degree of urbanization in China from 1980 to 2022", Statista, January 2023, https://www.statista.com/statistics/270162/urbanization-in-china/.

4   Zeping Ren, Xiaotong Li, and Yanxue Hua, "How Chinese Fell Out of Love with Marriage," *Caixin*, March 22, 2021, https://asia.nikkei.com/Spotlight/Caixin/How-Chinese-fell-out-of-love-with-marriage.

5   Helen Davidson, "Chinese Province Ends Ban on Unmarried People Having Children," *The Guardian*, January 30, 2023, https://www.theguardian.com/world/2023/jan/30/sichuan-province-in-china-removes-all-birth-restrictions.

6   The new civil code in 2021 makes divorce more difficult. It stipulates that before a divorce application can be approved, couples have to wait for thirty days to "cool off" and reconsider their decision.

7   Carlos Barria, "China to Reduce Abortions for 'Non-medical Purposes,'" *Reuters*, September 27, 2021, https://www.reuters.com/world/china/china-says-will-reduce-number-abortions-non-medical-purposes-2021-09-27/.

8   Xi Jinping, "Xi Jinping on Family Values," *Xinhua News*, May 9, 2021, http://www.xinhuanet.com/english/2021-05/09/c_139933730.htm.

9   Siqi Ji, "Chinese Couples Still Reluctant to Have 3 Children Despite Policy Shift, Surveys Show," *South China Morning Post*, December 29, 2022, https://www.scmp.com/economy/china-economy/article/3204944/chinese-couples-still-reluctant-have-3-children-despite-policy-shift-surveys-show.

10 "How LGBTQ Life in China Has Gotten Tougher under Xi," Bloomberg News, April 27, 2022, https://www.bloomberg.com/news/articles/2022-04-27/how-lgbtq-life-in-china-has-gotten-tougher-under-xi-quicktake.

11 Eli Friedman, *The Urbanization of People: The Politics of Development, Labor Markets, and Schooling in the Chinese City* (New York: Columbia University Press, 2022).

12 Yige Dong, "Does China Have a Feminist Movement from the Left?" *Made in China Journal* 4, no.1 (2019): 58–63.

13 Tian Feng, "Sit, Eat, Wait for Death: Life in the Shenzhen Sticks," *Sixtone*, September 8, 2020, https://www.sixthtone.com/news/1006145/ sit%2C-eat%2C-wait-for-death-life-in-the-shenzhen-sticks.

14 Zheng Wang, *Finding Women in the State: A Socialist Feminist Revolution in the People's Republic of China, 1949–1964* (Berkeley: University of California Press, 2019).

15 "China Women's Rights Centre Closes amid Civil Society Crackdown," Reuters, February 1, 2016, https://www.reuters.com/article/uk-china-rights-women/china-womens-rights-centre-closes-amid-civil-society-crackdown-idUKKCN0VA2CC.

16 Catherine Tucker and Yudan Pang, "Chinese Activists Are Using Blockchain to Document #MeToo Stories," *Harvard Business Review*, October 30, 2018, https://hbr.org/2018/10/ chinese-activists-are-using-blockchain-to-document-metoo-stories.

17 Angela Xiao Wu and Yige Dong, "What Is Made-in-China Feminism (s)? Gender Discontent and Class Friction in Post-socialist China," *Critical Asian Studies* 51, no. 4 (2019): 471–92.

18 Yige Dong, "The Dilemma of Foxconn Moms: Social Reproduction and the Rise of 'Gig Manufacturing' in China," *Critical Sociology* 49, nos. 7/8 (2022): 1231–49, https://doi.org/10.1177/08969205221140927.

19 For women workers contributing to and sacrificing for China's COVID battle, see "Women Workers on the Frontline in the Battle against the Coronavirus," *China Labor Bulletin*, March 5, 2020, https://clb.org.hk/ content/women-workers-frontline-battle-against-coronavirus; for migrant workers' resistance, see the high-profile case of Foxconn: Eli Friedman, "Foxconn's Great Escape," *Asian Labor Review*, November 8, 2022, https://labourreview.org/foxconns-great-escape/; Promise Li and Yige Dong, "The Foxconn Uprising in Zhengzhou," *Tempest*, December 5, 2022, https://www.tempestmag.org/2022/12/the-foxconn-uprising-in-zhengzhou/; for the suffering of the ethnic minorities, see the incident in Ürümqi, see Ashley Smith, "Resisting Genocide: The Uyghur Struggle for Justice: An Interview with Rayhan Asat," *Spectre*, February 8, 2023, https://spectrejournal.com/resisting-genocide-the-uyghur-struggle-for-justice/; for the victimization of the elderly and the sick, see, for example, "China: Treatment for Non-Covid Illnesses Denied," Human Rights Watch, April 6, 2022, https://www.hrw.org/news/2022/04/06/ china-treatment-non-Covid-illnesses-denied.

20 Lu Shen and Liyan Qi, "In China, Young Women Become Accidental Symbols of Defiance," *Wall Street Journal*, January 25, 2023, https://www.

wsj.com/articles/in-china-young-women-become-accidental-symbols-of-defiance-11674667983.

Chapter 5: China's National Questions

1   Arif Dirlik, "Born in Translation: "China" in the Making of 'Zhongguo'," *boundary 2: an international journal of literature and culture* 46, no. 3 (2019): 121–52.

2   Emily T. Yeh, *Taming Tibet: Landscape Transformation and the Gift of Chinese Development* (Cornell: Cornell University Press, 2013).

3   Margaret Maurer-Fazio, "Ethnic Discrimination in China's Internet Job Board Labor Market, " *IZA Journal of Migration* 1 (2012): 1–24.

4   Gerald Roche, James Leibold, and Ben Hillman. "Urbanizing Tibet: Differential Inclusion and Colonial Governance in the People's Republic of China." *Territory, Politics, Governance* 11, no. 2 (2023): 394–414.

5   Jiaojiao Sun and Yanjun Xie. "The 'Internal Orientalism': New Encounter in Tibet Tourism," *Current Issues in Tourism* 23, no. 12 (2020): 1480–92.

6   International Campaign for Tibet, updated April 6, 2022. https://savetibet.org/tibetan-self-immolations/.

7   Darren Byler, Ivan Franceschini, and Nicholas Loubere, *Xinjiang Year Zero* (Canberra: ANU Press, 2022).

8   "The Xinjiang Data Project," Australian Strategic Policy Institute. https://xjdp.aspi.org.au/.

9   Ilham Tohti, *We Uyghurs Have No Say: An Imprisoned Writer Speaks* (New York: Verso Books, 2022).

10 Darren Byler, *Terror Capitalism: Uyghur Dispossession and Masculinity in a Chinese City* (Durham: Duke University Press, 2021).

11 Helen Davidson, "Xinjiang Births Plummeted after Crackdown on Uyghurs, Says Report," *The Guardian*, May 12, 2021, https://www.theguardian.com/world/2021/may/12/chinese-uyghur-policy-causes-unprecedented-fall-in-xinjiang-birthrates.

12 Xinjiang Victims Database, https://shahit.biz/eng/.

13 Ho-fung Hung, *City on the Edge: Hong Kong under Chinese Rule* (Cambridge: Cambridge University Press, 2022).

14 Editors, "Almost Nobody in Hong Kong under 30 Identifies as 'Chinese'," *The Economist*, August 26, 2019, https://www.economist.com/graphic-detail/2019/08/26/almost-nobody-in-hong-kong-under-30-identifies-as-chinese.

15 Ming-sho Ho, *Challenging Beijing's Mandate of Heaven: Taiwan's Sunflower Movement and Hong Kong's Umbrella Movement* (Philadelphia: Temple University Press, 2019).

16 Jono Thomson, "TSMC Founder Unsettled by Talk of Labor Unions Building US Plant," *Taiwan News*, July 5, 2023, https://www.taiwannews.com.tw/en/news/4936730.

17 Finbarr Bermingham, "Chinese Envoy to France Lu Shaye Doubles Down on Taiwan 'Re-education' Aims," *South China Morning Post*, August 8,

2022, https://www.scmp.com/news/china/diplomacy/article/3188192/
chinese-envoy-france-lu-shaye-doubles-down-taiwan-re-education.

Chapter 6: The US v. China

1   "Madrid Summit Declaration," North Atlantic Treaty Organization, June
    29, 2022, https://www.nato.int/cps/en/natohq/official_texts_196951.htm.

2   *National Security Strategy*, White House, December 2017, https://
    trumpwhitehouse.archives.gov/wp-content/uploads/2017/12/NSS-
    Final-12-18-2017-0905.pdf.

3   For an introduction to this understanding of imperialism, see Phil Gasper,
    Imperialism and War: Classic Writings by V. I. Lenin and Nicolai Bukharin
    (Chicago: Haymarket Books, 2017).

4   Alex Callinicos, *Imperialism and Global Political Economy* (Cambridge:
    Polity Press, 2009), 137–227.

5   David McNally, *The Global Slump* (Oakland: PM Press, 2011), 25–60.

6   "Victory Not an Option," *Talk of the Nation*, National Public Radio,
    February 22, 2007, https://www.npr.org/2007/02/22/7551119/
    general-victory-not-an-option-in-iraq.

7   See McNally, *Global Slump*, and Michael Roberts, *The Long Depression*
    (Chicago: Haymarket Books, 2016).

8   David Wallace-Well, "What Can Replace China as a Global Economic
    Engine?," *New York Times*, August 23, 2023, https://www.nytimes.
    com/2023/08/23/opinion/columnists/what-can-replace-china-as-a-global-
    economic-engine.html.

9   Ho-fung Hung, *Clash of Empires: From "Chimerica" to the "New Cold War"*
    (Cambridge: Cambridge University Press, 2022), 47.

10 Daisuke Wakabayashi and Claire Fu, "China's Biggest Homebuilder Reels
    as Economy Slows," *New York Times*, September 4, 2023, https://www.
    nytimes.com/2023/09/04/business/china-country-garden-debt-crisis.html.

11 Aaron L. Friedberg, *A Contest for Supremacy: China, America, and the
    Struggle for Mastery in Asia* (New York: W. W. Norton & Company, 2011),
    88–119.

12 Ashley Smith, "US Imperialism's Pivot to Asia," *International Socialist
    Review*, 88, https://isreview.org/issue/88/us-imperialisms-pivot-asia/index.
    html.

13 Helene Cooper, "US Defense Secretary Supports Trade Deal with Asia,"
    New York Times, April 6, 2015, https://www.nytimes.com/2015/04/07/us/
    politics/defense-secretary-supports-trade-deal-with-asia.html.

14 Barry R. Posen, "The Rise of Illiberal Hegemony: Trump's Surprising
    Grand Strategy," *Foreign Affairs*, March/April 2018, https://www.
    foreignaffairs.com/united-states/rise-illiberal-hegemony.

15 Patrick McGee, "How Apple Tied Its Fortunes to China,"
    Financial Times, January 17, 2023, https://www.ft.com/content/
    d5a80891-b27d-4110-90c9-561b7836f11b.

16   Wolf Richter, "GM's Business Is booming in China," *Business Insider*, December 6, 2017, https://www.businessinsider.com/ gms-business-is-booming-in-china-2017-12.

17   "Blue Dot Network," US Department of State, https://www.state.gov/ blue-dot-network/.

18   Ashley Smith, "Illiberal Hegemony: The Trump Administration's Strategy for US Imperialism," *International Socialist Review* 109, https://isreview. org/issue/109/illiberal-hegemony-trump-administration-strategy-us-imperialism/index.html.

19   Ashley Smith, "The Bitter Fruit of Trump's China Bashing," *Socialist Worker*, February 24, 2019, https://socialistworker.org/2019/02/24/ the-bitter-fruit-of-trumps-china-bashing.

20   Robert Malley and Phillip H. Gordon, "Trump Still Has 70 Days to Wreak Havoc around the World," *New York Times*, November 11, 2020, https://www.nytimes.com/2020/11/11/opinion/biden-trump-foreign-policy.html.

21   Katrina Manson, Aime Williams, and Michael Peel, "What Does a Biden Presidency Mean for the World?," *Financial Times*, January 19, 2021, https://www.ft.com/content/75592d75-61ec-43f2-b435-c760db86394a.

22   Joseph Biden, *Interim National Security Strategic Guidance*, March 2021, https://nssarchive.us/wp-content/uploads/2021/03/2021_Interim.pdf.

23   Chun Han Wong, "Biden Imposes First Sanctions on Chinese Officials Ahead of Bilateral Meeting," *Wall Street Journal*, March 17, 2021, https:// www.wsj.com/articles/biden-imposes-his-first-sanctions-on-chinese-officials-ahead-of-bilateral-meeting-11615976219.

24   Edward Wong and Ana Sawanson, "US Aims to Expand Export Bans on China over Security and Human Rights," *New York Times*, July 5, 2022, https://www.nytimes.com/2022/07/05/us/politics/us-china-export-controls.html.

25   Jim Tankersley and Michael Shear, "Biden Signs Executive Order Bolstering 'Buy America' Provisions," *New York Times*, January 25, 2021, https://www.nytimes.com/2021/01/25/us/politics/biden-buy-american. html.

26   Thomas Hummel, "We Need Better Than the Inflation Reduction Act," *Tempest*, August 24, 2022, https://www.tempestmag.org/2022/08/ we-need-better-than-the-inflation-reduction-act/.

27   Chris Miller, *Chip War: The Fight for the World's Most Critical Technology* (New York: Scribner, 2022).

28   Phil Mattingly, "Biden Signs Executive Order Kick-Starting Implementation of Sweeping US Chip Manufacturing Law," *CNN*, August 22, 2022, https://www.cnn.com/2022/08/25/politics/chip-manufacturing-biden-executive-order/index.html.

29   Kathie Lobosco, "Here's What's in the Bipartisan Semiconductor Manufacturing Package," *CNN*, August 9, 2022, https://www.cnn.

com/2022/08/09/politics/chips-semiconductor-manufacturing-science-act/index.html.

30   Don Clark and Anna Swanson, "US Pours Money into Chips, but Even Soaring Spending Has Limits," *New York Times*, January 1, 2023, https://www.nytimes.com/2023/01/01/technology/us-chip-making-china-invest.html.

31   Anna Swanson and Edward Wong, "With New Crackdown, Biden Wages Global Campaign on Chinese Technology," *New York Times*, October 13, 2022, https://www.nytimes.com/2022/10/13/us/politics/biden-china-technology-semiconductors.html.

32   Peter Baker and David Sanger, "Biden Orders Ban on New Investments in China's Sensitive High-Tech Industries," *New York Times,* August 9, 2023, https://www.nytimes.com/2023/08/09/us/politics/biden-ban-china-investment.html.

33   Maegan Vasquez, "Biden Signs Vital $858 Billion Defense Bill into Law," December 23, 2022, https://www.cnn.com/2022/12/23/politics/biden-signs-ndaa/index.html.

34   Aamer Madhani, "US, Japan, South Korea to Announce Deeper Defense Cooperation at Camp David Summit," ABC4.com, August 14, 2023, https://www.abc4.com/news/politics/ap-politics/ap-us-japan-south-korea-to-announce-deeper-defense-cooperation-at-camp-david-summit/.

35   Connor M. Savoy and Shannon McKeowen, "Opportunities for Increased Multilateral Engagement with B3W," Center for Strategic and International Studies, May 6, 2022, https://www.csis.org/analysis/opportunities-increased-multilateral-engagement-b3w.

36   Anna Cooban, "Europe Unveils Its $340 Billion Answer to China's Belt and Road Infrastructure Initiative," CNN Business, December 1, 2021, https://www.cnn.com/2021/12/01/business/global-gateway-eu-china-belt-road/index.html.

37   Ido Vock, "Stab in the Back: How the New Aukus Pact Sparked French Outrage," *New Statesman*, September 16, 2021, https://www.newstatesman.com/world/2021/09/stab-in-the-back-how-the-new-aukus-pact-sparked-french-outrage.

38   "The 2021 Summit for Democracy," Freedom House, https://freedomhouse.org/report/summit-democracy/2021/summit-democracy-ratings-scores.

39   Peter Baker and Zolan Kanno-Youngs, "Biden to Begin New Asia-Pacific Economic Bloc with a Dozen Allies," *New York Times*, May 31, 2022, https://www.nytimes.com/2022/05/23/world/asia/biden-asian-pacific-bloc.html.

40   Julie Zhu, "Exclusive: China Readying $143 Billion Package for Its Chips Firms in Face of US Curbs," Reuters, December 13, 2022, https://www.reuters.com/technology/china-plans-over-143-bln-push-boost-domestic-chips-compete-with-us-sources-2022-12-13/.

41   Paul Mozur and John Liu, "With Ban on Micron, China Microchip Clash with U.S.," *New York Times*, May 22, 2023, https://www.nytimes. com/2023/05/22/business/micron-technology-china-ban.html.

42   Annabelle Liang and Nick Marsh, "Gallium and Germanium: What China's New Move in Microchip War Means for World," BBC, August 2, 2023, https://www.bbc.com/news/business-66118831.

43   Peter S. Goodman, "Why Chinese Companies Are Investing Billions in Mexico," *New York Times*, February 3, 2023, https://www.nytimes. com/2023/02/03/business/china-mexico-trade.html.

44   Diego Lopes da Silva, Nan Tian, Lucie Béraud-Sudreau, Alexandra Marksteiner, and Xiao Liang, "Trends in World Military Expenditure, 2021," SIPRI, April 2022, https://www.sipri.org/sites/default/ files/2022-04/fs_2204_milex_2021_0.pdf.

45   Associated Press, "China Upgrades Its Naval Force with Its First Indigenous Aircraft Carrier," NPR, June 17, 2022, https://www.npr.org/2022/06/17/1105786322/ chinas-upgrades-its-naval-force-with-its-first-indigenous-aircraft-carrier.

46   Amy Hawkins and Helen Davidson, "China May Be Planning Overseas Naval Bases in Asia and Africa, Say Analysts," *The Guardian*, July 27, 2023, https://www.theguardian.com/world/2023/jul/27/ china-building-overseas-naval-bases-across-asia-and-africa-say-analysts.

47   Helen Cooper, "China Could Have 1,000 Nuclear Warheads by 2030, Pentagon Says," *New York Times*, November 3, 2021, https://www. nytimes.com/2021/11/03/us/politics/china-military-nuclear.html.

48   Dave E. Sanger and William J. Broad, "China's Weapon Test Close to a 'Sputnik Moment,' US General Said," *New York Times*, October 27, 2021, https://www.nytimes.com/2021/10/27/us/politics/china-hypersonic-missile.html.

49   Lingling Wei and Stella Yifan Xei, "China's 40-Year Boom Is Over. What Comes Next?," *Wall Street Journal*, August 20, 2023, https://www.wsj. com/world/china/china-economy-debt-slowdown-recession-622a3be4.

50   Michael Karadjis, "Ukraine War: Sub-Imperialist Posturing, Not 'Anti-colonial' Resistance, behind the Neutrality of Reactionary Elites in the Global South," *Syrian Revolution Comment and Analysis*, January 13, 2023, https://mkaradjis.com/2023/01/13/ukraine-war-sub-imperialist-positioning-not-anti-colonial-consciousness-behind-the-neutrality-of-reactionary-elites-in-the-global-south/.

51   James Kynge, "China's Blueprint for an Alternative World Order," *Financial Times*, August 22, 2023, https://www.ft.com/ content/8ac52fe7-e9db-48a8-b2f0-7305ab53f4c3.

52   Doug Palmer, "As Tensions Rise, U.S. Imports from China Plummet," *Politico*, August 8, 2023, https://www.politico.com/news/2023/08/08/ us-china-imports-drop-00110243.

53   David J. Lynch, "U.S. Companies Are Buying Less from China as Relations Remain Tense," *Washington Post*, August 6, 2023,

https://www.washingtonpost.com/business/2023/08/06/
us-china-economy-trade-mexico/.

Chapter 7: China and Global Capitalism's Ecological and Climate Crises

1   The Intergovernmental Panel on Climate Change, *IPCC Sixth Assessment Report*, 2021, https://www.ipcc.ch/report/ar6/wg1/downloads/report/IPCC_AR6_WGI_Headline_Statements.pdf.

2   "China Emissions Exceed All Developed Nations Combined," BBC, May 7, 2021, https://www.bbc.com/news/world-asia-57018837.

3   Steven Mufson and Brady Dennis, "Chinese Greenhouse Gas Emissions Now Larger than Those of Developed Countries Combined," *Washington Post*, May 6, 2021, https://www.washingtonpost.com/climate-environment/2021/05/06/china-greenhouse-emissions/.

4   "China's Coal Share of Energy Consumption Falls in 2020, but Overall Coal Use Up," Reuters, February 28, 2021, https://www.scmp.com/economy/china-economy/article/3123464/chinas-coal-share-energy-consumption-falls-2020-overall-coal.

5   "China Generated over Half World's Coal-Fired Power in 2020: Study", Reuters, March 29, 2021, https://www.reuters.com/article/us-climate-change-china-coal-idUSKBN2BK0PZ.

6   Tess Riley, "Just 100 Companies Responsible for 71% of Global Emissions, Study Says," *The Guardian*, July 10, 2017, https://www.theguardian.com/sustainable-business/2017/jul/10/100-fossil-fuel-companies-investors-responsible-71-global-emissions-cdp-study-climate-change.

7   Christoph Nedopil Wang, *China Belt and Road Initiative (BRI) Investment Report H1 2021*, International Institute of Green Finance (IIGF) of the Central University of Finance and Economics (CUFE), China, July 27, 2021, https://green-bri.org/china-belt-and-road-initiative-bri-investment-report-h1-2021/.

8   Peng Yin, Michael Brauer, Aaron J. Cohen, et al, "The Effect of Air Pollution on Deaths, Disease Burden, and Life Expectancy across China and Its Provinces, 1990–2017: An Analysis for the Global Burden of Disease Study 2017," *Lancet*, August 17, 2020, https://www.thelancet.com/journals/lanplh/article/PIIS2542-5196(20)30161-3/fulltext.

9   Richard Smith, *China's Engine of Environmental Collapse* (London: Pluto Press, 2020).

10   Binbin Wang and Qinnan Zhou, "Climate Change in the Chinese Mind: An Overview of Public Perceptions at Macro and Micro levels," *WIREs Climate Change* 11, no. 3, (May/June 2020), https://wires.onlinelibrary.wiley.com/doi/10.1002/wcc.639.

11   Jeff Tollefson, "COVID Curbed Carbon Emissions in 2020—but Not by Much," *Nature*, January 15, 2021, https://www.nature.com/articles/d41586-021-00090-3.

Chapter 8: Pandemics in an Epoch of Imperial Rivalry

1   Global Preparedness Monitoring Board, *A World at Risk: GPMB 2019 Annual Report*, September 18, 2019, https://www.gpmb.org/reports/annual-report-2019.

2   John Gertner, "You Should Be Afraid of the Next 'Lab Leak,'" *New York Times*, November 23, 2021, https://www.nytimes.com/2021/11/23/magazine/covid-lab-leak.html.

3   Dhruv Khullar, "Lab Leaks and COVID-19 Politics," *The New Yorker*, March 3, 2023, https://www.newyorker.com/news/daily-comment/lab-leaks-and-Covid-politics.

4   Heran Zheng and Shixiong Cao, "Threats to China's Biodiversity by Contradictions Policy," *Ambio* 44, no. 1 (February 2015): 23–33, https://www.ncbi.nlm.nih.gov/pmc/articles/PMC4293358/.

5   Evelyn Cheng, "Virus Disclosure in China Was Delayed Because Disease Control Group Lacks Authority, Top Scientist Says," CNBC, February 2020, https://www.cnbc.com/2020/02/28/chinas-cdc-lacks-authority-to-alert-public-on-virus-scientist-says.html.

6   "He Warned of Coronavirus. Here's What He Told Us before He Died," *New York Times*, February 2020, https://www.nytimes.com/2020/02/07/world/asia/Li-Wenliang-china-coronavirus.html.

7   "Mutual Aid and the Rebuilding of Chinese Society," Lausan, July 2020, https://lausancollective.com/2020/mutual-aid-and-the-rebuilding-of-chinese-society-part-1/.

8   "Social Contagion: Microbiological Class War in China," *Chuang*, February 2020, https://chuangcn.org/2020/02/social-contagion/.

9   Eli Friedman, "Escape from the Closed Loop," *Boston Review*, November 2022, https://www.bostonreview.net/articles/escape-from-the-closed-loop/.

Chapter 9: "China" in the US

1   "National Report," Stop AAPI Hate, September 2021, https://stopaapihate.org/national-report-through-september-2021/.

2   This chapter will mainly be focused on Chinese Americans but will also make reference to the experiences of other Asian Americans when relevant.

3   "Key Questions," Chinese Railroad Workers in North America Project at Stanford University, https://web.stanford.edu/group/chineserailroad/cgi-bin/website/faqs/.

4   Ling Li and Biao Teng, "An Anatomy of Trump's Appeal to Chinese Liberals: A Conversation with Teng Biao," *Made in China Journal*, February 1, 2021, https://madeinchinajournal.com/2021/02/01/an-anatomy-of-trumps-appeal-to-chinese-liberals-a-conversation-with-teng-biao/.

5   China has become the US's largest debtor (rising to the top in 2008 and dropping to the second since 2016), and the US trade deficit with China grew from $83 billion in 2000 to $355 billion in 2021 (with a peak value of $418 billion right before the trade war). See "U.S. Trade with China",

US Bureau of Industry and Security, 2021, https://www.bis.doc.gov/index.php/country-papers/2971-2021-statistical-analysis-of-u-s-trade-with-china/file#:~:text=In%202021%2C%20U.S.%20exports%20to,from%20%24310.3%20billion%20in%202020.

6   Foreign students studying at US higher education institutions is counted on the balance sheet as education exports. John Bound, Breno Braga, Gaurav Khanna, and Sarah Turner, "The Globalization of Postsecondary Education: The Role of International Students in the US Higher Education System," *Journal of Economic Perspectives* 35, no. 1 (2021): 163–84.

7   While the number of Chinese students in the US remained relatively small in earlier years, it kept growing at a double-digit rate from fewer than 60,000 in 2000 to 372,000 in 2019. Despite political turmoil and COVID-related restrictions, there are still more than 300,000 Chinese students studying in US colleges and universities at the present.

8   "Chinese Students Are Valued in the US, Says US Assistant Secretary of State," ICEF Monitor, August 14, 2019, https://monitor.icef.com/2019/08/chinese-students-are-valued-in-the-us-says-us-assistant-secretary-of-state.

9   "A Bloomberg News analysis of the 50 indictments announced or unsealed since the start of the program and posted on the Justice Department's China Initiative web page reveals a further problem: The China Initiative hasn't been very successful at catching spies. The largest group of cases, 38% of the total, have charged academic researchers and professors with fraud for failing to disclose affiliations with Chinese universities. None of them has been accused of spying, and almost half of those cases have been dropped. About half as many Chinas Initiative cases concern violations of US sanctions or illegal exports, and a smaller percentage involve cyber intrusions that prosecutors attributed to China. Only 20% of the cases allege economic espionage, and most of those are unresolved. Just three claim that secrets were handed over to Chinese agents." Sheridan Prasso, "China Initiative Set Out to Catch Spies. It Didn't Find Many," Bloomberg, December 14, 2021, https://www.bloomberg.com/news/features/2021-12-14/doj-china-initiative-to-catch-spies-prompts-fbi-misconduct-racism-claims.

10   Elizabeth Redden, "A Retreat from China Collaborations in the Face of U.S. Scrutiny," *Inside Higher Ed*, October 29, 2021, https://www.insidehighered.com/news/2021/10/29/survey-finds-chilling-effect-china-initiative.

11   "White Paper on 2021 International Education in China," Hurun Report, March 22, 2022, https://www.hurun.net/en-US/Info/Detail?num=ECIPDLTFKYHJ.

12   This has been reflected in recently published research by the sociologist Yingyi Ma. See Yingyi Ma, *Ambitious and Anxious: How Chinese College Students Succeed and Struggle in American Higher Education* (New York: Columbia University Press, 2021).

13 "International Students: Fields of Study by Country of Origins,"
    Institution of International Education, 2022, https://opendoorsdata.org/
    data/international-students/fields-of-study-by-place-of-origin/.

14 Jacob Feldgoise and Remco Zwetsloot, "Estimating
    the Number of Chinese STEM Students in the United
    States," Center for Security and Emerging Technology,
    October 2020, https://cset.georgetown.edu/publication/
    estimating-the-number-of-chinese-stem-students-in-the-united-states/.

15 For some reports on this, see: Sritama Chatterjee, "Benefits of a Graduate
    Students' Union for International Students in the U.S.," *Inside Higher Ed*,
    November 26, 2019, https://www.insidehighered.com/blogs/gradhacker/
    benefits-graduate-students%E2%80%99-union-international-students-us;
    Michael Sainato, "US Graduate Students Protest against Low Pay While
    Universities Profit from Their Work," *The Guardian*, March 30, 2022,
    https://www.theguardian.com/us-news/2022/mar/30/us-graduate-
    students-protest-against-low-pay-while-universities-profit-from-their-work.

16 "Organizing from below: Chinese International Student Workers and the
    UC Strike," Lausan Collective, January 31, 2023, https://lausancollective.
    com/2023/chinese-student-workers-uc-strike/.

17 "About Us", https://www.csanetwork.org/about-us

18 For details, see CSA's homepage: https://csanetwork.org/.

Conclusion: Neither Washington Nor Beijing

1   See Cornell University School of Industrial and Labor Relations, "Labor
    Action Tracker," https://striketracker.ilr.cornell.edu/.

2   JS Tan, "Tech Workers Are Workers, Too," *Jacobin*, May 6, 2019, https://
    jacobin.com/2019/05/tech-workers-chinese-solidarity-microsoft-github.

3   For more groups and publications, see "Suggested Readings and
    Resources" at the end of the book.

INDEX

labor laws, 15, 57
labor movements, 57–59 passim, 172, 175; Taiwan, 96. *See also* strikes; unions
labor NGOs, 57, 59
Labor Notes, 172
labor unions. *See* unions
Lam, Carrie, 90
landownership, 24–25, 48–50
land seizure, 24, 47–52 passim, 65
lawsuits, 72
LGBTQ people, 67; same-sex marriage, 95
Li Wenliang, 143, 144
Liu Jingyao, 72
Liu Qiangdong, 72
Llasa uprising, 1959, 80, 82

Ma, Jack, 33, 38, 117
Malaysia, 36, 40, 42
Malley, Robert, 111
manufacturing statistics, global, 123
Mao Zedong, 28–29, 30, 127
"mass incidents," 48, 56
#MeToo movement, 72
Mexico, 118, 166
microchips, 37–38, 43, 113, 114, 117–18
migrant children, 68, 70
migrant workers: internal, 14–16, 31, 51–58 passim, 64; riots, 18; Vietnamese, 25. *See also* guest worker programs
migration, rural–urban. *See* rural–urban migration
migration to the United States, 152–53
militarization and militarism, 6–7, 36, 41–42, 98–100 passim, 114, 122, 147; high-tech industry and, 114, 121; United States, 41–42, 109, 110–11, 114, 118, 122
military technology, 37
Miller, Chris, 113

minorities, ethnic. *See* ethnic minorities
Muslims, 83–87 passim
Myanmar, 40, 41, 168

nationalism, 38, 165–68. *See also* ethnonationalism
National People's Congress (NPC), 19
National Security Law, 91
native peoples. *See* indigenous peoples
NATO, 103, 104, 106, 116, 117
navies: China, 118; United States, 36, 109, 110–11, 122
Netherlands, 114. *See also* Dutch colonialism
New Zealand, 40, 104, 114
nongovernmental organizations (NGOs). *See* environmental NGOs; feminist NGOs; labor NGOs
North Atlantic Treaty Organization. *See* NATO
nuclear submarines, 116, 119
nuclear weapons, 110, 118, 123

Obama, Barack, 109
Odom, William, 106
offshoring, 58, 118, 170
oil and oil industry, 21, 22, 106, 119, 120, 128
Olympic Games, Beijing, 2008, 82
Olympic Games, Beijing, 2022. *See* Winter Olympic Games, Beijing, 2022
Ou, Howey, 133

Pakistan, 36, 40, 41–42, 118
Palestine, 24, 120
pandemics. *See* epidemics and pandemics
Paris Climate Agreement, 128
patriarchy, 68, 71
peasants, 29, 31, 64, 78; land dispossession and resistance, 24, 47–52 passim, 65; rural

ABOUT HAYMARKET BOOKS

Haymarket Books is a radical, independent, nonprofit book publisher based in Chicago. Our mission is to publish books that contribute to struggles for social and economic justice. We strive to make our books a vibrant and organic part of social movements and the education and development of a critical, engaged, and internationalist Left.

We take inspiration and courage from our namesakes, the Haymarket Martyrs, who gave their lives fighting for a better world. Their 1886 struggle for the eight-hour day—which gave us May Day, the international workers' holiday—reminds workers around the world that ordinary people can organize and struggle for their own liberation. These struggles—against oppression, exploitation, environmental devastation, and war—continue today across the globe.

Since our founding in 2001, Haymarket has published more than nine hundred titles. Radically independent, we seek to drive a wedge into the risk-averse world of corporate book publishing. Our authors include Angela Y. Davis, Arundhati Roy, Keeanga-Yamahtta Taylor, Eve L. Ewing, aja monet, Mariame Kaba, Naomi Klein, Rebecca Solnit, Mohammed El-Kurd, José Olivarez, Noam Chomsky, Winona LaDuke, Robyn Maynard, Leanne Betasamosake Simpson, Howard Zinn, Mike Davis, Marc Lamont Hill, Dave Zirin, Astra Taylor, and Amy Goodman, among many other leading writers of our time. We are also the trade publishers of the acclaimed Historical Materialism Book Series.

Haymarket also manages a vibrant community organizing and event space in Chicago, Haymarket House, the popular Haymarket Books Live event series and podcast, and the annual Socialism Conference.

ALSO AVAILABLE FROM HAYMARKET BOOKS

BRICS: An Anticapitalist Critique
Edited by Patrick Bond and Ana Garcia

China on Strike: Narratives of Workers' Resistance
Edited by Eli Friedman, Zhongjin Li, and Hao Ren

*Dying for an iPhone: Apple, Foxconn,
and The Lives of China's Workers*
Jenny Chan, Pun Ngai, and Mark Selden

*The New Cold War: The United States,
Russia, and China from Kosovo to Ukraine*
Gilbert Achcar

*Striking to Survive: Workers' Resistance
to Factory Relocations in China*
Fan Shigang, introduction by Sam Austin and Pun Ngai

To Govern the Globe: World Orders and Catastrophic Change
Alfred McCoy

Twilight Prisoners: The Rise of the Hindu Right and the Fall of India
Siddhartha Deb

ABOUT THE AUTHORS

Kevin Lin is a researcher focusing on labor and employment relations, collective actions, and civil society in China. He is based in Hong Kong.

Rosa Liu is a writer and activist based in China.

Eli Friedman is associate professor and chair of international and comparative labor at Cornell University's ILR School. He is the author of *Insurgency Trap: Labor Politics in Postsocialist China* and coeditor of the English edition of *China on Strike: Narratives of Workers' Resistance*. He splits his time between the US and China.

Ashley Smith is a socialist writer and activist in Burlington, Vermont. His writing has appeared in numerous publications including *Truthout*, the *International Socialist Review*, *Socialist Worker*, *Jacobin*, *New Politics*, *Against the Current*, and many other online and print publications.